Tales of a Path

By A. L. Westgard

Originally published by A. L. Westgard
Copyright 1920, by A. L. Westgard, Published March 1920
Copy republished by AGG Publications, 2013©

Note on A.L. Westgard written by Terri Horvath

All photos were not included in the original book.

Dedication by Westgard: To my wife, who has shared with me the hardships as well as the pleasures of the trail, ever a cheerful comrade and a trusty adviser.

Note on A.L. Westgard

By Terri Horvath

"I confine myself to the safe statement that I have made more motor trips across the United States, East and West, North and South, than any other man, and that these trips were mostly over different routes."—
A.L. Westgard

By the time this book was published, Anton L. Westgard had traveled thousands of miles to charter the way west for the automobile to follow. He became a celebrity known for his trailblazing efforts. Some people saw him as the "Daniel Boone of the Gasoline Age," "John the Baptist of the Good Roads Gospel," or "The Great Pathfinder of the Good Roads Era,"

He did indeed endure life-threatening blizzards, scarcity of gasoline, and blinding dust storms among other obstacles to his mission.

Today we see his contribution as little more than a footnote in the history of automotive travel, but he deserves greater acknowledgement. Westgard was one of the pioneers who helped build the foundation for the automotive travel.

I discovered the name of Westgard while working on another book, *Hoosier Tour: A 1913 Indiana to Pacific Tour*. While pouring over this material, I realized that these men, particularly Westgard, were pioneers in their own right. They had indeed risked hardships in the early days of automotive travel. The idea was a revelation to me, and I thought it should be shared.

The following pages are Westgard's own story and impressions as he wrote them in 1920.

He died in 1921.

Foreword

The story of the highways is the story of mankind, where in a state of barbarism or of civilization. The movement of primitive peoples has been by waterways and land-routes which, following lines of least resistance, often appropriated the trails made by wild animals. The movements of civilized men likewise followed the least resistive lines with the result that the great railways and the national highways coincide with the game-trails and the Indian paths of long ago.

The ascent of man has been in direct ratio to the progress that has been made in the speed, safety, comfort and convenience of the movement of men and goods from one place to another.

The wheel is the emblem of human progress. The supreme evolution of the wheel is the automobile.

Already six and a half million automobiles are daily employed in speeding a third of the population of the United States along their way with the demand increasing so rapidly that the factories are unable to meet it.

Every intelligent citizen in the United States knows that the next big job for America now that the war is over is to construct road beds as perfectly adapted to the economic operation thereon of motor vehicles as the road bed of the railway is adapted to the use thereon of its rolling stock. The two and a half million miles of roads in the United States will be made modern highways as rapidly as the work can be financed and the men and material secured for the purpose. The strength of the States and the counties will be put forth in increasing measure until this result is secured. The Federal Government has already placed the zero milestone in Washington to designate the point from which a system of National highways will extend clear to the surf-beat of the Pacific and from lands of snow to lands of sun. The Federal Government, the States and the Counties are working out a system of National, State and County highways, the most important of which will be the first improved. The creation of such a system of highways will do more for the welfare and advancement of the people of the United States, more for the unity, security, development and glory of the Nation than could possibly be accomplished by a like expenditure of money and energy in any other line of endeavor.

If this be true, what is the measure of the debt of gratitude which the public owes to the apostles of better roads and to the men who have pioneered the ways that are now to become the great National Thoroughfares. Among the latter, chief indeed of the Pathfinders, is the author of this volume, A. L. Westgard. The year 1903 saw him driving his first car on the roads of New York. Since then he has been the constant explorer of the ways that lead from east to west, from north to south, inspecting, mapping, publishing, making men know and appreciate what a country this is; urging the delights of the open road and the life of the great outdoors. Almost all of the more than forty great highways along lines of latitude and longitude follow the trail of his pathfinding car—or cars—for he has worn out eighteen cars in this work. His services in this interest have made him a benefactor of humanity.

If, as I believe, the most important fact for Americans is America, the main part in the education of an American citizen is to know America. This book is a direct contribution to this end.

Dr. S. M. Johnson
March, 1920
Roswell, New Mexico and Washington, D.C.

By Way of Explanation

The days of the pathfinder of motor-car routes are about over. With few exceptions the routes that may become trunk-line highways are already beaten paths of known quality and future work in connection with routes will concentrate on improving surface conditions.

It has been contended that the pathfinder's work of the past has been an important factor in the development of the good roads movement and consequently of the automobile and allied industries, and it is in response to frequent urgings of my many friends within these industries that this book was written.

A. L. Westgard

Chapters

The Trundle Wheel

When I was a young man, I was employed by a publishing house engaged in issuing State, county and city atlases and maps all over the United States. In the county atlases the maps covered towns or townships and villages. The property dimensions along country roads, especially in the Eastern States, where the section system of dividing land into units of a mile square did not prevail, were obtained by the use of the so-called trundle wheel. This consisted of a large, very light wooden wheel, with two long handles reaching from the hub, and by the means of these the contrivance was pushed along country roads. The diameter of the wheel was about five feet. The revolutions of the wheel were measured on an odometer at the hub, and the circumference in feet multiplied by the number of revolutions of the wheel would give the distance covered between points. On the handles was fastened a plane-table with compass attached, to get the proper bearings of the road at bends and turns.

While the trundle wheel may seem a crude contrivance, it worked with great accuracy, but it was no lazy man's job to push it along from twenty to thirty miles a day and work out the bearings, mark the property lines, their lengths and courses, as well as the location of the houses along the road, on the map on the plane-table, besides stopping to get the name of the owner of each property. I have covered thousands of miles footing it along country roads in this manner and this was my initiation into pathfinding work. The wide scope of the work also gave me a rather intimate knowledge of roads and soil conditions in many widely separated sections of the country. This knowledge was further amplified upon the arrival of the pneumatic-tired bicycle, which, as the railroads did to the canals, superseded the trundle wheel and relegate it to a historic past.

Then followed the automobile. While in the early days of motordom as much time was probably spent under the car tinkering as in the driver's seat, the trundle wheel in comparison to the modern automobile is as the prehistoric ruins in our Southwest compared to modern city skyscrapers. From the trundle wheel to the bicycle and to the automobile I used progressively the means at hand and seem to have grown into pathfinding work. It has been very interesting work too. The preparation of dependable route maps all over the United States has in no small measure helped in their development and the desire to travel over them. The main routes have by reason of their known quality as first learned through the medium of the pathfinder's work become the standardized routes of today. The travel induced over certain main lines, as a consequence of the work of the pioneer pathfinder, has in turn caused improvements running into the hundreds of millions of dollars, to be followed by billions or more dollars as time rolls on. The pathfinder's work, beginning with the trundle wheel, will thus be seen to have been the very foundation stone, the very first beginning of the good-roads movement which now has taken such an impetus that unquestionably a system of nationally built and maintained highways will be constructed as a framework for the thousands of miles of roads which will be built by states and counties to supplement them as feeders.

I feel no small pride for having had the privilege and opportunity to help in the pioneer pathfinding work which has borne such magnificent fruit. While I am now counted the veteran of the guild I am as keenly as ever watching the development along all the main trunk lines of the country and doing my humble share in helping to keep up the interest in sections where lethargy may show too healthy signs. Incidentally I count the year lost that I cannot personally inspect the progress of work on at least two of the standard transcontinental lines. Eighteen transcontinental trips and more than that many between the North and South boundaries of the United States on rubber tires are behind me and I am still going.

The Desert Tramp

We left Yuma one bright morning to inspect the route up the Fila Valley, which is now distinguished beyond that of any other in the United States, because in spite of its desert character, it is an important link in four distinct Transcontinental routes, viz.: the Dixie Overland Highway, the Bankhead Highway, the Southern National Highway and the Old Spanish Trail, besides figuring as a link in the Borderland Trail.

However, at the time of our trip here concerned none of these promotions had been conceived and, as then there was no bridge across the Gila River at Antelope Hill, it was necessary to ferry or ford across the Gila at Dome Station and follow a rather uncertain desert trail via Castle Dome and Middle Well, joining the route as now laid out at Las Palomas. We had expected to reach Aguas Calientas, where there were primitive accommodations for travelers, before dark, but owing to very rough and chucky trail between Yuma and Dome and some slow going near Middle Well darkness overtook us before we reached Las Palomas.

As we had no commissary we decided to push on to Aguas Calientas in spite of the lateness of the hour. The country was dotted with giant Saguaro cactus and creosote bushes which took on all sorts of weird shapes in the glare of our acetylene headlights. About ten o'clock it seemed to me that I saw some moving object far ahead and thought it was probably a skulking coyote, but as we forged ahead our headlights picked up a man walking towards us along the dim path.

As the sport was miles from any habitation it was hard to believe one's eyes, as certainly no sane person would brave this barren and desolate arid country on a mere hike. That would be gambling with death in too reckless a fashion. As we drew near we noticed that the man was weaving sideways or stumbling ahead like a drunken person. He eventually stopped as we were a couple of hundred feet distant and fell prone on the ground.

On reaching him I jumped off the car and bent over his prostrate body and only then realized that here was one of those terrible cases where a human had almost succumbed to the grasp of the desert. He was about all in from thirst. Filling a cup from our canvass water bag I fed water to him a drop at a time and as he gradually regained strength had to use physical force for prevent him from gulping down the entire contents of the cup at one draught. The wonder of a few drops of the life-giving fluid!

Eventually he was strong enough to give us his story or at least what was purported to be his story. Three days previously he had left Las Palomas, which by the way was only some ten miles distant, in search of a prospector's camp which he had been told was only a dozen miles at the side of a mountain plainly visible from Las Palomas. It may be well to state here that Las Palomas is not a settlement but merely a desert trading store catering to the occasional prospectors who with their outfits and burros roam over the desert in search of the El Dorado which is always expected to be discovered tomorrow. He had failed to locate the camp and had utterly lost his sense of orientation, wandering haphazardly about without knowing where he was headed. He had had nothing to eat since leaving Las Palomas and only the one pint bottle of water while his suffering from the daytime heat of the desert was, if anything, only increased by the cold of the nights which penetrated his poorly clad body.

In spite of his terrible experience and narrow escape from madness and probable death he insisted that he would continue his search for the camp if we would only fill his bottle with water. Whether this was an example of foolhardiness or grit, or possibly fear of civilization with its officers of law I do not know, but no amount of persuasion on our part could induce him to abandon his intentions.

After teaching him to find the north star and indicating the exact direction of Las Palomas we filled his water bottle, presented him with our canteen full of the precious moisture, and as we cranked up our car to proceed he snuggled under a creosote bush for a nap.

Ever since that day I have often wondered if we saved his life only to have him lose it possibly in some remote canyon of that wonderfully fascinating desert country or if he found his camp, helped to work the riches from the ground and today is possibly one of those who enjoy the prosperity in some large city, which his evident education clearly fitted him to appreciate under happier circumstances.

Optimism

In tracing the Midland Trail, now the Roosevelt National Highway, across the United States, we passed through Western Kansas in the month of July during a time of terrible drought. Truly this was a benighted country that season. First the grasshoppers, or "hoppers" as the settlers call them, had eaten every green leaf in the cornfields, which only a week or two previous had by their fine stand aroused such glowing hopes of a bounteous harvest, leaving only the bare stalks and making the fields look as though some crazy person had raised a crop of beanpoles.

On top of this came one of those dreaded hot winds out of the north which feels like a blast out of a furnace and wither all growing things to wilted shreds in a few days. Then the grasshoppers returned and as there was nothing else left finished the job by eating the cornstalks, which they had scorned on their first visit when green vegetation was plentiful. These insects would fly in swarms and would soon become plastered on the front of the radiator of our car in such numbers as to prevent the fan from drawing air through it necessitated frequent stops to scrape their charred bodies off with a stick. Besides our windshield had to have frequent cleaning of the juices of their battered bodies as we met in head-on collisions. When one hit us in the face the force of the impact would cause considerable pain as though we were hit by a pebble.

As may readily be imagined the appearance of the country looked so hopeless and dispiriting as to make one wonder why anyone had ever had the temerity and courage to ever settle there or at least to continue living in a region where fortune could ordinarily be counted on to favor one with her smiles only once in five or six years. With these thoughts in mind I stopped at one of the homesteads which seemed if possible more afflicted and utterly barren than the rest.

A man came out on the porch followed by a woman who, from natural curiosity to know what the strangers wanted, came to the door to listen to the conversation. In place of woebegone expression of despair I was certainly rather taken aback by the genial good-natured smile which met my greetings. After a few remarks about the proposed highway I cautiously offered my sympathy about the hardships incident on the failure of the crops. Instead of receiving in return a long tale of woe the farmer passed it off as a matter of only passing moment, maintaining that they were pretty sure to get one good crop in five and that the one good crop every fifth year brought larger net returns than five mediocre crops in the East and he thanked his God that he was not cramped by too close neighbors—and in fact he was glad he lived in God's country, viz.: Western Kansas. An opinion to which his good wife nodded a smiling agreement.

If there is a more sunny optimist on the face of this green earth than a West Kansas farmer I would like to meet him.

In 1912, Westgard encountered this covered wagon traveling the same road as he near Big Springs, NE.

The Cow and the Route Book

The next year after I laid out the "Ideal Tour" of New England a general publicity tour over the route was organized and several of the automobile editors of the New York daily papers were invited to take part in the junket. There were some twenty cars in the caravan and everything went well with everybody enjoying the beautiful country and the good hotels even though in those early days before the era of paved highways the roads failed to come up to their present standard of excellence.

At one particularly scenic spot in New Hampshire a stop was made by the roadside in order to allow everyone the opportunity to enjoy the wonderful view, and a couple of the newspaper men strolled along the road a little way. One of these men was known for his droll sayings and dry wit, the kind that is uttered without the suspicion of a smile though it generally brought a roar of appreciation from those that heard his witty words.

A short way down the road these two men noted a farmer just across the fence struggling to tie a board in front of a cow's face, a performance that was difficult in view of the fact that the poor bovine had no horns to which to fasten the board. The other newspaper man, not the witty one, was a city-bred chap and immediately wanted to know from the farmer why he attempted to practice such cruelty on his cow, the most useful animal on earth. In fact he grew quite irate and upbraided the farmer rather severely. After listening in silence for a while to this tirade the farmer informed him that it was necessary to tie the board in front of the cow's eyes in order to prevent her from seeing and thus finding weak spots in the fence through which to make her way into the neighbor's fields and damage the crops growing there.

This true and reasonable answer seemed to satisfy the humane newspaperman when our droll wit pulled one of the route-information books, which were universally used in those days, out of his pocket and handing it to the farmer said most seriously: "The board is cruelty to animals. Tie this to her neck and if she can find her way anywhere with that she deserves a feed in your neighbor's fields," then turned on his heel and without a trace of a smile returned to the waiting cars.

Marooned

While making the original survey of the Northwest Trail, later called the National Parks Highway, we left New York in the middle of June and arrived at Glendive in the Yellowstone River Valley in Montana with fair speed, after some rather painful experiences with North Dakota mosquitoes, as related in another chapter, and after crossing the Little Missouri river at Medora, N.D., on the railroad bridge. It will be remembered that Medora is the little town at the edge of the "Bad-lands" where Col. Theodore Roosevelt punched cattle when a young man and incidentally received the inspiration to write of the West.

As we proceeded up the Yellowstone Valley, along the historic path of many a doughty pioneer, trapper, Indian and soldier we learned of floods in the upper reaches of the river, caused by the melting snows of the Rocky Mountains. Having had a rather hazardous experience in crossing the Powder River, as told elsewhere, we pitched camp one night at a ranch house, which was located on a knoll near the lonesome station of Zero. There was more than irony in that name.

When we awoke next morning we were located on an island, the knoll being entirely surrounded by floodwater from the river which flowed nearby. The rancher assured us that there was no cause for apprehension as he had had this experience in June every year of the three years he had lived there and that the water would subside in a couple of days at most. In the meantime the water was still rising and our island gradually growing smaller while the shores seemed to grow more distant hourly.

However we felt reassured by the rancher's confidence and proceeded to have as good a time as the circumstances would allow. As our commissary was practically empty when we reached this locality, it having been our intention to replenish it at Miles City, we were dependent on the rancher and his good wife for meals and we were very hospitably made to feel that we were welcome to share whatever their larder afforded. The continual rising of the water caused us considerable anxiety and I noted that the rancher was not altogether easy in his mind. Near dusk it seemed that the flood had about reached the peak and though our island by that time seemed mighty small we retired for the night with the feeling that it would have grown to much greater size by morning. In this expectation we found ourselves disappointed when daylight revealed about the same condition as the night before.

All day we watched the flood racing by carrying trees, logs, sheds and small houses and by night time there seemed to be no appreciable diminution in the stage of the water. We had by then become so used to the idea of being marooned that the familiarity with the strange and fascinating spectacle of the raging waters, as well as with the possible danger of our situation, had in some degree blunted our fears. The following morning the waters were a trifle higher than the night before, our island was now not over an acre in extent.

While eating breakfast at the ranch house that morning I got the impression that it seemed comparatively scant in volume and the housewife evidenced considerable anxiety while serving us. However these manifestations were not sufficiently pronounced to leave a lasting remembrance and were soon forgotten in the more important business of watching the flood. On the fourth day the waters showed only a barely appreciable diminution and the housewife confessed to being out of flour for bread, the flood having caught them just as they were about to lay in a new supply of food of various kinds, which had in fact reached the railroad station but had not yet been hauled home.

The situation now became more serious as there was no other food available except some chickens and three or four turkeys. On the seventh day the chickens were all eaten and how we did hate chickens, fried, stewed or otherwise prepared, by the time the last was consumed. After the first turkey things seemed indeed dark, just fowl without potatoes, bread or biscuits, became as bad as the proverbial mule of civil war time when the choice in some army camps rested between fried, roasted, stewed or jerked mule days on end.

To our great relief and pleasant surprise we had on the tenth day for breakfast a dish of delicious white meat which seemed exceedingly palatable after the continuous diet of fowl. Our curiosity was intense to know what it was and whence if came. After much persuasion the rancher told us he had been lucky enough to catch a couple of prairie dogs, which had been driven out of the flooded underground apartment, and wasn't it lucky? Well, maybe it was, but the expression on the faces of us three Easterners did not seem to indicate that we appreciated our luck. Especially my wife seemed to show an utter lack of appreciation of this good fortune if one could judge by the woebegone expression on her face.

We were marooned on this Robinson Crusoe island sixteen days in all, and eventually after arduous struggles across soggy river flats succeeded in piloting our car into Miles City. And it may be believed that bread and butter and coffee and pie, and then some more bread and butter, tasted like the manna and ambrosia of the Gods! And then to top it all off—a pipe of blissful smoke. Chickens, offered in any style whatsoever, had no attraction for us for several years after.

A.L. Westgard is photographed (far right) in front of his car while traveling the National Old Trails Road.

A Modern Noah's Ark

On one occasion while inspecting the route which later became the famous River-to-River road across Iowa, we failed on account of slow and heavy going, to reach the town where we had planned to spend the night, and as my car always, even nowadays when en route, carries a camping outfit, we pulled into a school-house yard to pitch camp for the night. As there usually is good drinking water, a supply of wood and other conveniences available in country school-house years, they were and are now favorite camping places in the West and this particular yard was especially inviting because it was level and smooth and was carpeted with a thick even crop of grass.

After having erected the tent and sitting down to our supper a boy came riding into the yard, made a tour of inspection and disappeared down the road at a lively gallop.

Shortly he reappeared accompanied by a team hauling an immense wagon built like a house, with doors and curtained windows and painted gaily like a gypsie wagon, also by another smaller wagon behind which a cow was tied with a short rope. This caravan pulled into the yard and stopped a few feet from our camp. Shortly the most wonderful collection of animate things appeared. Besides the four horses and the cow there came from those wagons two hogs, two goats, four geese, three ducks, a half dozen chickens, six dogs of various sizes and breeds, a cat, a monkey and a parrot, in fact the wagon proved a veritable Noah's Ark.

After stretching their cramped limbs these various species of the animal kingdom proceeded to inspect the premises and showed a special fondness for inspecting our camp and its equipment. The boss of this outfit was a tremendous giant of a woman who assured us that her animals were merely curious and asked us not to mind them, which advice was easier to give than to follow. The squawk of ducks, hissing of geese, crowing of cocks, grunting of hogs, barking of dogs and chattering of the parrot and the monkey furnished a veritable bedlam of noises while the woman, her male hired hand and the boy proceeded to milk the cow and the goats, attend to the horses and get their camp ready.

Everything was done with dispatch as each had his particular task to perform, and in an hour's time everything was properly tucked away for the night, even the animals seemed to know by long training, exactly what was expected of them.

Now came the time for a visit over the campfire and the woman proved a very interesting talker, recounting her many varied experiences on the road. She was what is called in the West a "drifter," that is a person who is never satisfied to stay long enough in one place to become a part of the community. She had roamed this way over the West for many years, a sort of self-sufficient and self-reliant tramp, making a living by trading lace and embroideries to farmer's wives and occasionally trading some livestock and varying this legitimate "business" by telling fortunes whenever she found a gullible specimen. Within her limitations and requirements she said she managed to get along, felt free to come and go wherever the fancy dictated and to "be her own boss and owe nobody a debt either of money or gratitude." She was a shrewd philosopher of the native sort.

Next morning we got started by the time her "crew" were harnessing their horses and we parted with her assurance that she would run across us again somewhere between the Alleghenies and the Rockies.

No Gasoline—and Yet

On my first trip into the Apache country I had been assured that if I could only reach Springerville, gasoline would undoubtedly be found at that settlement. We left McCarthy station on the Santa Fe railroad and cut across country on faint trails meandering across mountains, between lava beds and cliffs, using mountain peaks as guiding landmarks, and finally after ninety miles of the roughest kind of going, unfit for wagons, let alone motor cars, made Nations' Ranch with the gasoline tank almost empty and with more than forty miles yet to go to Springerville. As luck would have it a few gallons of the precious fluid were found at the ranch, where it had been kept for a pumping engine and this enabled us to reach Springerville. My motor car, or "outfit," as the local people called it, was the first ever seen in this Mormon settlement, located so far from a railroad.

Mr. Becker, the local merchant, who was later destined to become the greatest power for the Good-Roads movement in Eastern Arizona, thought I would surely be able to procure gasoline at Fort Apache, sixty miles further in the heart of the wild and exceedingly rough country of the Mogollon and White Mountains. As no motor car had ever before visited the region, it seemed foolhardy, I was told, to attempt to reach the army post over the execrable trails across the volcanic plateau of the White Mountains, over nine thousand feet high. However, if I dared to undertake it the merchant was willing to give me the gasoline contained in the store-lamps, the only supply in the settlement. This scant supply coupled with the stories about the country ahead did not promise well, but nevertheless we started out. The ascent of the mountains proved exceedingly arduous and so slow that we were overtaken by darkness and worse yet by a blizzard (it was in November) by the time we reached half way across the plateau. More than half frozen after a tough tussle with snowdrifts, cold blasts, buried lava boulders and lost trail, we arrived towards dawn at Cooley's Ranch, forty-two miles out, the only house on the way.

After being thawed out and having partaken of a substantial breakfast we finally arrived at Fort Apache and found unbounded hospitality but no gasoline. Here was a serious situation. At the time there was only a small troop of cavalry with three officers at the post and these three were very glad to see somebody from "the outside," especially if that somebody would make a fourth hand at whist. Chatting about the gasoline situation between deals I was offered all sorts of sympathy, but as this would not move motor cars it seemed there was nothing to do but sit down and wait for a team to go to Holbrook on the railroad for a supply, and freighters took two weeks for a round trip to that point.

During the game the captain's "boy," a Filipino, came into the room for some uniforms that were hanging in a closet. He inspected these carefully and left the room with them. Asking the captain where the boy was going with the clothes at that time of night I was answered that he was to remove some spots from them. Struck by an idea I suddenly came to life with a new hope and asked to be permitted to talk with the boy. He was called and was much surprised at my curiosity regarding what he used for removing the spots. He said he used a cleaning fluid which he got from the post quartermaster. In spite of the late hour the quartermaster was sent for and admitted having four or five gallons of this "cleaning fluid" in stock. Next morning this very fluid made the engine frisky as a colt and the contents of the quartermaster's "cleaning fluid" container enabled me to reach Globe, sixty miles distant and the incident had become a mere experience of the trail.

Nowadays gasoline and all sorts of motor car supplies are procurable at a number of places along the same route and a good cinder road crosses the White Mountains plateau, while thousands of cars pass through Springerville every season—and it is only nine years since my first trip into this region.

Frenchman's Station

One moonbright midsummer's evening our party arrived at Frenchman's Station, located in the most arid part of Central Nevada near the trail that in former days was the Pony Express route and two generations later became the Lincoln Highway. The station was kept by a Frenchman who made a living by hauling water from a spring, twelve miles distant, and selling it to freighters hauling ore and supplies between mining camps to the South and the railroad at Eureka. He also had sleeping accommodations in one of the two rooms in his cabin and furnished meals to travelers.

As the hour was late and my wife somewhat tired, we thought that, rather than take the time to pitch the tent and prepare camp, we would look over the accommodations of the station. I was deputized to examine these and report. I found that the double iron bedstead in the "guest room" occupied every inch of space necessitating undressing in the other room or perform the feat in the bed somewhat in the manner necessary in a Pullman berth. The facts were promptly reported back to the car.

Friend wife thought she had better have an individual peep and after looking the situation over thought it would do if the host would furnish clean linen. After having this cryptic word explained to him as meaning clean sheets and pillow cases he rolled his eyes and sputtered a flow of protestations assuring us that we need have no worry about the linen as the people who slept in that bed last were perfectly clean people, in fact as he put it: "as clean as Bill Taft." Mr. Taft at that time was our President.

Eventually we succeeded in inducing the production of satisfactory bedding and proceeded out into the lean-to shed of a kitchen in anticipation of something to eat. Here my wife discovered a luscious-looking watermelon partly covered by a wet cloth to keep it cool and at once made a requisition on a generous slice. Our host, however, held up his hands in protest and with many apologies maintained that to grant this request would be out of the question and entirely impossible as he had had it brought all the way from Reno in anticipation of the visit of the "great pathfinder" who was expected over the route on an inspection trip as stated in the Reno papers and this was intended as a pleasing surprise to the great man. To encounter a luscious watermelon in the most arid part of Nevada, a hundred miles from a railroad, would be sure to convince him that after all this route had its advantages and should be advocated as a National touring boulevard and thus bring lucrative business to the station.

When my wife asked who this great man was he produced a copy of a Reno newspaper a few days old which contained an account of the expected visit of her husband. The half-tone photograph accompanying the article was taken when I wore city clothes and thus he had not recognized me. We chose not to enlighten him and enjoyed a fair meal sans watermelon. Our host in the meantime volubly set forth his bright prospects of future profits from travel over the expected boulevard. He was so earnest and enthusiastic that we did not have the heart to discourage him.

Now on the door of my car was a small brass plate on which was engraved my name and official position. Next morning when I went out to the car to see if everything was all right, I found the watermelon on the tonneau floor covered by the wet cloth but our host was nowhere in sight. In fact we prepared our own breakfast and only when we were ready to depart did he come from behind a nearby small hill and with tears in his eyes uttered his profound mortification over the fact that he had not recognized me, and his hopes that I would not let "this unfortunate demonstration of his absurd stupidity" influence me against locating the boulevard past his station.

While the boulevard is still only on the maps this route has attracted such a share of the transcontinental motor traffic that it is safe to assume that our host is reconciled for the lack of the boulevard by the increased flow of revenue from the tourist traffic. At least I hope he is as he was a cheerful, good old soul, residing alone out there in the barren and burning desert.

Faculty of Orientation

While making the pioneer motor survey up the Yellowstone Valley in Montana, over what is now the National Parks Highway and also the Yellowstone Trail, we arrived, after a hard tussle with flooded river flats, at the little town of Custer. Here I found that further progress up the valley was out of the question on account of the flood, so began investigating the possibility of working out a way around through the hills to the south. I was told there was an old trail along the crest of Pine Ridge, in view some miles to the south, and that I might be able to find a way up to the crest of this ridge, though no one seemed to know where a trail went up or was willing to venture an opinion as to whether a motor car would be able to attain the summit up the apparently steep side slopes.

However, to sit still was not on the program, so we started for the hills with eyes anxiously scanning them from afar in an effort to discover what might prove a path or trail of some kind. We drove across country along sheep trails and across them till we came to the first foothills without having discovered any sign of a trail up the slopes. We did find, however, that the ridge was deeply incised by small canyons or gashes and after having carefully inspected several of these on foot, I thought I saw the possibility of reaching the top of the ridge by zig-zagging up the rather sharply inclined side of one of these canyons. In making our way up through the gravelly dry bed of the canyon we soon found that we could not get out of this bed to gain the firmer ground of the side hill, in fact we were soon so firmly imbedded in the loose gravel that we would move neither forward or backwards, and realized that it would be the arduous work of many hours to extricate the car from its position.

Before entering the canyon or "draw" as it is called in Montana, I had noticed the white canvas of a sheep-wagon some two or three miles distant on the rolling foothills. To enlighten the uninitiated a sheep-wagon is the home-on-wheels of a sheep herder. This home is moved from one location to another about every two weeks to provide new grazing grounds for his flock of about two thousand sheep which he has in charge for the owner, who may own from ten to sixty of these sheep-wagons and who brings a team of horses for moving them from one location to another when required.

In order to avoid the arduous work of getting the car out I took our driver Heinie out to the edge of the draw and pointed out to him the location of the sheep-wagon and asked him to go over there to see if he could procure the use of a team, cautioning him to note well the location of the canyon in order to find his way back to our car. Now Heinie had the faculty of losing his way more prominently developed than anyone I ever met, in fact his bump of orientation was so dwarfed that he would lose his way back to the hotel of a city if the garage were around the corner and thus out of sight of it. Hence my cautioning him not to miss the particular canyon in which our car was when he returned from the sheep-wagon with or without the horses, especially in view of the fact that the car was down in a depression and could not be seen unless one came within a couple of hundred feet of it.

Next morning at an anxious and hasty breakfast Heinie was still missing and the worst was that I did not think it well to leave my wife alone in camp in order to go and hunt for the boy, as one of the Indian sheep-herders might pay our camp a visit. All the morning I scanned the surrounding country with the field glasses and finally about two o'clock, twenty-four hours after his leaving the car, I spied him afar off coming towards the ridge accompanied by a man driving a team of horses. Much relieved I hurried down to the car and reported to my wife that Heinie was in sight and to help get something ready for him to eat in case he was hungry. The meal about ready, I again went up on the slight elevation from where I had seen the party approaching, but Heinie and his companion had disappeared and were nowhere in sight nor, in spite of shots fired, shouts and waving of red blankets, could we discover any further sign of them for the rest of the entire day. Another anxious night was spent in camp and Heinie was still missing the next noon. However, two hours later he again appeared in the focus of the field glasses still accompanied by his friend with the horses, and this time I took no chances of losing him again, but ran out to meet them about a mile from the car.

Heinie started out assuring me he would be back in a jiffy and we could hear his merry whistle grow fainter as he drew away into the distance. I started to make a fire to prepare a bit to eat as friend wife suggested we should have everything ready against Heinie's return so as to be prepared to move promptly. This was about two o'clock in the afternoon. In the course of an hour or a little more I went out of the draw to look for Heinie, but he was nowhere in sight. We waited all the long afternoon and still no Heinie. We were beginning to get considerably worried about the boy, particularly when I saw through the field glasses that the sheep-herder was preparing his supper and that he was alone at his camp. I fired a couple of shots to attract Heinie's attention in case he was lost and roaming over the side of the ridge. As no answering cry resulted we finally prepared our camp for the night and had a good fire burning, thinking that the glare of the flames might guide the boy back.

Poor Heinie had had a hard time of it. When he reached the sheep-wagon he found it deserted, but spied another one a mile or so beyond and here he found willing folks with a team who was glad to be of help. But alas, when Heinie undertook to act as guide back to the car he stared in blank amazement at the ridge. Every canyon and gash looked alike to him and there were literally hundreds of them. So they spent forty-eight hours hunting for the right one, with poor Heinie worried sick. He was surely a happy boy to get to the wheel of his beloved car again.

The team yanked us out of our troubles in no time, and after several attempts in various localities we finally attained the summit of the ridge. That was indeed some ride along the hog-back crest of Pine Ridge, crossing saddles and rifts, and when, by evening, we finally succeeded in finding a way down on the other side of the ridge we were a mighty tired lot in camp that night. Next day we made Miles City via Harder and found that they were organizing searching parties to go and look for us as our departure from Custer three days before had been promptly chronicled in the city papers and our arrival that first night had been expect. It was thought that we had met with an accident in the hills or that we might have been murdered by renegades.

Yuma Border

Before the construction of the highway bridge at Yuma it was nothing unusual for motorists, who reached the ferry on the California side after six o'clock P. M., to have to spend the night in their cars as the ferryman could not be hired, threatened or otherwise persuaded to break his rule not to work after hours, no matter what the hardships to the tourists, who were compelled to sit there in the dark, generally supperless, too, and watch the blinking arc lights of the city of Yuma just across the river, and not a wide river at that.

Having had this experience on two separate occasions, I put the matter up to the city authorities and the movement for the building of a highway bridge connecting the convenient bluffs just above the ferry, already discussed as a possibility of the future, took on added impetus. Concrete action followed. By the cooperation of the Federal government with the States of Arizona and California, the bridge was built—and the ferryman lost his job as he fully deserved.

A Mormon Dance

On one of my trips from Zuni to Inscription Rock our party spent the night at the small Mormon settlement of Ramah and that evening were invited to attend a dance at the place which served as schoolhouse, house of worship and public meeting house generally. When a fair-sized crowd had assembled, the fiddler tuned up and the merry-makings ready to start, the elder or whatever he is called in the Mormon church, arose and asked everybody to join in prayer. Like many a deacon of other faiths he proceeded to give the Lord a lot of information, which he seemed to think the Supreme Power should know about and finally asked that evil thoughts be kept from the dancers.

Some of the young men in my party, who had been introduced generally among the young ladies, had evidently missed an introduction to two or three of them and when they asked for a dance were promptly turned down by these because they were not properly introduced. A strict observance of the conventions were demanded even in this isolated and remote region. The festive occasion was closed with another long prayer.

Westgard is photographed in front of his Pathfinder 40 in 1913.

A Mexican Wedding

Entering on one occasion an all-Mexican village in Arizona we were met by a wedding procession. Preceded by two musicians, one playing a guitar and one a violin, the white-dressed bride, led by the hand of the groom, came towards us with measured and stately strides. Following were the relatives of the happy pair, all with beaming faces and chatting animatedly.

As we drove to one side to make room for the procession the groom halted its march, came over to our car and handed me a written invitation to attend a dance with refreshments that evening at the house of the bride's father. Presumably this invitation was extended to all strangers encountered during the progress of the procession. Surely a convincing proof of the great hospitality of these unlettered simpleminded folk, this extending a friendly hand of welcome to whoever enters their gates.

The Yuma Mummy

As a proof of the dryness of the desert air, I will relate an experience I encountered in Yuma, even though the joke, somewhat ghastly, was on myself.

One of chief boosters for creating motor tourist traffic to and through the town was the city undertaker. The president of the local automobile club escorted me over to the undertaking establishment to introduce me, and finding no one in attendance in the office left me there, with an apology, to go in search of the proprietor. I sat down in a chair, and after idly glancing through a magazine which told all about coffins and shrouds, I looked up and my eyes saw reflected in a mirror on the opposite wall, a man standing in the corner of the room behind my chair. And if a face could ever portray the definition of a diabolical grin this man's certainly did. To say that I was startled is putting it mildly. I am afraid I arose from that chair with a bound, surely with an alacrity frowned upon in the best social circles where deliberateness is a distinguishing mark. Facing the man with the grin I was astounded to note that it was a grin that refused to come off, it was there for keeps.

Upon closer inspection this ghastly apparition proved to be a mummified human with long hair streaming down alongside his sunken face, and gleaming white teeth glistening brightly. Heavy eyebrows and some of the tousled hair hid its eyesockets. It was fully dressed and standing almost straight in the corner of the room, leaning only slightly against one wall. No wonder I was startled.

Upon the arrival of the undertaker I was told this body had stood there in the corner of the room for more than a year, and that it was found out on the desert. The dry air prevented decay and merely turned the deceased into a mummy. No one seemed to know anything of the man who met this luckless fate. It was many a day before I forgot this experience.

Notorious

In 1911 the Glidden Tour was run from New York to Jacksonville in the month of October. As I was to start on a route investigation trip to California near the beginning of October, I did the pathfinding for the Glidden Tour in the latter part of August, arriving in Jacksonville the first week in September.

Owing to pressure of time I travelled fairly fast for a strictly pathfinding tour, especially when considering the fact that careful strip maps were made of the route as we went along, besides notes of hotel accommodations for the big crowd to follow on the Glidden Tour. This did not give us much time for the many various entertainments usually attendant upon a tour of this kind, especially where cities on two parallel possible routes were bitterly and jealously contending for the honor of being chosen as a noon or night stop for the big tour. Many unique arguments were often brought forth in such cases. I think that pathfinding as a whole, considering the delicate task of choosing only one, and that the best one, of several competitive optional routes without causing hard feelings or worse, is the best possible training for a man qualifying for the diplomatic service.

However, I could not altogether avoid entertainments which were staged to show me honor or to influence my judgment in the choice of routes as the case might be. These occasions were usually attended by more or less speech-making—usually more. I was frequently presented to the assemblage in terms most extravagant as the greatest pathfinder since Daniel Boone and General Fremont. At one place I was called the "Daniel Boone of the Gasoline Age," at another "John the Baptist of the Good Roads Gospel," or "The Great Pathfinder of the Good Roads Era," and similar flattering phrases.

But it remained for the mayor of one of the smaller Georgia towns to cap the climax. In the center of the public square was the usual band stand, and when our car arrived with all its occupants, grimy from a combination of dust and perspiration. I was escorted up the steps of the stand, around which the majority of the citizens of the town were assembled. After the mayor had made some rather lengthy and not altogether apropos remarks to the people he told them that they should feel especially honored that auspicious day in having among them such a man as myself. Beckoning me to come forward he exclaimed in a voice of thunder, heard all over the square: "Allow me to present to you, my fellow citizens, the most notorious tourist of the age." Just that. Of course the laugh was on me.

If I had not perfected my plans for another transcontinental trip it would have been my province to pilot the Glidden Tour over this route. As it was, my place was taken by one of my co-workers, an old and dear friend. Near the town where the mayor referred to me as the notorious, when he meant the notable tourist, the pilot car, running along a high speed, was ditched and the man who took my place as pilot was killed.

The photo illustrates typical conditions of roads in rural areas. This was a section of the Lincoln Highway looking west at 14.4 miles east of Indiana-Illinois state line (Courtesy of the LHA collection/University of Michigan)

The Padre's Prophesy

When on an inspection tour over the Pacific Highway from Seattle to San Diego we eventually approached Southern California, it was late in the year and the Southland beckoned us with promise of sunshine and good roads. Having entered upon El Camino Real, the old Kings Highway, which in early days was only a trail connecting the twenty-two Franciscan Missions of California and which now constitutes a link in the Pacific Highway, it was of course inevitable that we decided to pay a visit to all the old missions, most of them now merely ruins, along the way. It was also of course inevitable that the camera was used freely to make photographs of the venerable structures as a means to refresh our memories of these visits in later years.

Having had the most pleasant experiences all along the line and security some splendid snapshots, we eventually arrived at the Santa Ynez mission near Los Olivos. A few years previously this mission had lost its imposing tower, which had tumbled down in a storm, owing to erosion of its material of construction and general old age, so that the mission bell had been mounted on an unsightly scaffolding in the open place fronting the chapel entrance. I proceed at once to get busy with the camera and, having taken all the photographs which I desired, noticed a small placard fastened on the front of the chapel door.

Upon approaching to read the placard I found to my consternation that it was a polite request to visitors not to make photographs of the mission before first procuring the permission of the padre. I felt much mortified in having, though unintentionally, ignored the inhibition, especially as I noticed that the padre was watching our behavior from the porch of the mission house, attached to the chapel building. In order to make my excuses and set myself right with the padre, I stepped up to him and tendered apologies for my apparent disregard of his printed request. With a gracious smile he said it would be all right as he never knew a photograph which had been taken, without first securing the requested permission, to turn out anything but a failure.

I assured him, however, that I knew my camera and also knew that my film was fresh stock, so I had no fear of the results, but would be happy to be allowed the privilege of making a contribution to the church box in partial atonement for my oversight. While thanking me for this, he thought that the photographs nevertheless would turn out bad. After a few moments pleasant chat we parted the very best of friends.

When in the course of a few days the trip was finished, and I had secured photographs of every one of the missions on the route, the films were developed. Every exposure made was excellent— except those made at Santa Ynez. The film was good, fresh stock, because others on the same roll came out fine. Thus the padre's prophesy came true, as the Santa Ynez photographs were so fogged that it was barely possible to recognize the objects intended to be depicted.

Pesky Pests

To travelers beyond the fringe of civilization it is well known that the further north one reaches the bigger and more vicious the mosquitoes are and, it seems, also more plentiful. While the damp regions of the tropic and subtropic countries of course have their share of the pests it is said that the mosquitoes of Alaska and the swampy wooded regions of Canada surpass the warmer climates in the number, the insistent rapaciousness and venom of these insects which near the dusk of the evening sweep the country in literally dense clouds inflicting suffering and often death on animals and such human beings as are not prepared with veils, screens and special clothing to resist and render futile their onslaughts.

However, the sloughs and coulees of our northern prairie states, such as Minnesota, the Dakotas and Montana, also furnish excellent breeding places for a species of mosquito which I believe in genuine devilishness and ingenuity, undiluted poison and militant generalship prove worthy matches to their Canadian and Alaskan cousins and to compare with which, the well-known and much condemned New Jersey variety are as tame household pets. While traversing the North Dakota prairies in search of the most likely location for a transcontinental motor route into the northwest on one occasion we were approaching Bismarck, the state capital. We were still some twenty miles east of the city and were pushing on to reach a good dinner before dark when our trail leads us across a sort of dike over several reed-grown swamps or sloughs.

When about half way across this dike, which was probably a quarter of a mile long, our car skidded off to one side and barely escaped plunging into the ooze of the swamp.

As it was we were "stuck." While we were busily endeavoring to get the car back on to the crown of the dike it seemed to me that the sun suddenly went down and the dusk of evening at once settled on the surrounding country. Looking up from the manipulation of the jack handle I saw a dense black cloud arise out of the slough and slowly, as though wafted by a breeze, draw nearer to us. I did not realize the nature of the thing till untold millions of mosquitoes buzzed around us and dived for an unprotected spot of our arms, heads, faces and necks.

As it was absolutely essential to continue with the work of getting the car going we simply had to scrape the pests off by the handful whenever we had a hand free that could be spared for the purpose. When there was no more room for lodgement on the exposed parts of our bodies the insects would light on our clothing and proceed to bore until they struck blood.

When after some twenty minutes tussle we finally succeeded in getting the car under way again the swarm bloodthirstily pursued us for a while, but finally gave up the chase. By this time the poison injected into our systems was beginning to have serious effects. We suffered cruelly and scratched ourselves until the blood flowed. On approaching the city I, who seemed to suffer the least, possibly on account of my being a tobacco smoker, had to take the wheel from the driver, whose face had become so swollen from the poison that his eyes were fast becoming closed by their puffed condition. They were entirely closed in fact when we drew up in front of the hotel.

We were compelled to stay in the town for two days under medical care before we had sufficiently eradicated the poison from our systems to be able to proceed. We surely acquired a wholesome respect for the efficiency of Mr. Mosquito and in the future were properly supplied with veils and heavy gloves as at least a partial protection.

Good Fellows

While surveying the Meridian Road from Laredo on the Rio Grande, in Texas, to Winnipeg, Manitoba, Canada, which highway practically divides the United States in two equal parts, some of the Texans accompanied me in two cars in order to boost for the improvement of the route and to extend a hearty welcome for a winter visit into the Sunny South to the dwellers of the more northerly states through which we passed.

Of course our cavalcade was met by delegations of enthusiasts which came to extend to us the hospitality of whatever community we were approaching along the entire route. These hearty welcomes compensated in a large measure for the many trying experiences which we had with rough trails, lack of culverts, primitive ferries over considerable rivers, furnace-like hot winds from parching corn and wheat fields, dust and perspiration. However, it must be admitted it sometimes added seriously to our discomfort to travel for several miles through a dusty country into a town when we were sandwiched between many escorting cars in front and rear, thus compelling us to partake of a dust diet, blow north or blow south.

It has been my good fortune during my many years of pathfinding and investigation of routes throughout the United States to meet many men in public life. Among these I have had fifty-two governors of various states ride in my car during periods extending from only an hour or so up to a two weeks good-road's campaign, and with few exceptions I have found these state executives the best of fellows, clean-minded good sports, as ready to lend a hand at the shovel to get up on the tonneau seat and make a speech, and apparently as contented to roll up in a blanket beside the campfire after a supper of camp "vittles" as to retire to a sumptuous suite of hotel rooms after an elaborate banquet.

On this trip over the Meridian Road we arrived at a state line somewhere near halfway of the route and were met by the governor of the state, accompanied by a large welcoming delegation in a long string of automobiles. At the first town we came to, they had prepared quite a feast for us in the way of a barbecue lunch, where all the good things of the season was served in great plentitude to everyone present. The governor of course was the object of special solicitude of a committee which had been appointed to particularly look after his comfort. I was seated alongside the governor and was much amused at the worry displayed by this committee when the governor let all the good things like roast pig, roast turkey and attendant fixings pass by without helping himself. Finally an immense platter heaped high with steaming golden roasted ears of corn appeared and the governor took six of these and piled them on his plate, then calmly proceeded to eat with apparent relish.

Everybody watched him with great interest as he busied himself with this repast, which ordinarily would suffice for three men, and when in silence and without interruption he had eaten the corn off the six cobs he said that but for modesty's sake he felt almost like emulating the Irishman, who after eating the corn off a cob passed it to the waiter with the request that the chef "put some more beans on this stick," to which remark one of those sitting near enough to hear it suggested that evidently the committee had brought the governor to the wrong place, they should have brought him to the livery stable and not to the barbecue. This caused much merriment and the governor acknowledged the laugh was on him and confessed to an inordinate fondness for roasted corn, a fondness which he only dared indulge to the full when Mrs. Governor was not present to look after his diet.

Saladito

While we were taking the first truck across New Mexico over what was later called "The Trail to Sunset" but is now part of the National Old Trails road, we arrived one evening at a long low one-story building, lonesomely located on the adobe plain between the Datil Mountains and Rito Quernado in the Western part of Socorro county. As we had had a battle with mud on the plains all day, the crew was dog tired and not in a mood for erecting tents and doing the work attendant upon preparing camp for the night, cooking food, washing dishes, making beds, etc. For this reason the sight of this lonesome habitation was very welcome.

We found that the house was not the dwelling of a family but a sort of Mexican apartment house, and that its name was Saladito, because it was located near a small salty spring. Six families occupied the structure. Their respective apartments, which consisted of two rooms each, were not intercommunicating which necessitated going outside in order to enter the apartment of one of the neighbors. I learned that the house, which by the way was not at all unusual in some remote parts of New Mexico, was built in this manner in order to provide better protection against possible danger of Indian attacks, which in not so far distant days was ever to be reckoned with and even today was never to be reckoned with and even today was used as a dwelling place by so many families because the nearness of fellow human beings was a great comfort in such a remote region, especially as the men were away during the day attending their flocks of Angora goats from which they made a living.

We were fortunate enough to induce one of the housewives, who was a childless widow, to take us in and allow us the use of one of her two rooms and also to cook our meals for us, using our provisions in their preparation, as none of us had succeeded in acquiring the taste for Mexican cooking, usually strongly seasoned with red pepper. While our supper was being cooked I made a visit down along the line of the other apartments and found they contained thirty persons all told, none of whom could speak or understand a word of English. As I had a nodding acquaintance with Spanish, I was able to put us on a friendly basis with the inhabitants and found to my surprise that we occupied a veritable Noah's Ark. That historic menagerie scarcely contained more species of animals than Saladito.

Aside from the thirty human beings, of whom the larger number were children of varying ages, I was able to enumerate two burros, eight dogs, five cats, sixteen chickens, nine pigs, one Angora ram and seven Angora kids, all occupying the rooms in common and seemingly getting along amicably.

During the night it rained, and as New Mexico adobe is some problem to negotiate when wet, even with a light car, let alone a seven-ton truck heavily loaded, I decided it was good policy to stay where we were until the country dried up, and thus we spent two days at Saladito. We had not a dull moment. The people, their domestic life, their homes and points of view on ordinary everyday affairs, were as interesting to us as we were to them. Besides, we had a well-earned rest, which put our crew in better trim to tackle the hardships ahead. As I knew the country from having traversed it the year before, I realized that these hardships were greater than I dared divulge to the members of the crew, knowing that they would attack difficulties that were not anticipated, with greater cheerfulness than those about which they had heard and thus allowed their imagination to magnify. Of course there were no roads, merely trails often too narrow for vehicular traffic.

Price Canyon

I think I may justly claim the conception of the Midland Trail, now called the Roosevelt National Highway, as I had carefully studied out its alignment as well as given it a name two years before I undertook to trace it on the ground. With the cooperation of the Denver Chamber of Commerce we crossed the Rocky Mountains over Berthoud Pass, 11,300 feet high. This pass had never been crossed by an automobile before. Eventually we arrived at Grand Junction near the Colorado-Utah line, and here I found a condition which gave food for serious thought.

The trip from Grand Junction, a prosperous city in the heart of a wonderful fruit belt, to Salt Lake City, three hundred miles distant, had been attempted on several occasions by motorists but had never been accomplished, the rough country and absence of culverts or bridges across washes and ravines compelling the shipment of the car for a considerable distance in every case. Upon learning this and realizing that I should probably also fail to reach the objective, I arranged for a meeting of the chamber of commerce. At this meeting I explained the importance to the city of being located on a transcontinental trunk highway and especially on one with so many scenic attractions as the Midland Trail. I then called for volunteers to accompany me to Salt Lake City in their car, suggesting that three or four husky fellows occupy each car to enable us to surmount all obstacles by sheer physical strength, and thus learn the real condition of the proposed route and arrange for means to eliminate its drawbacks.

In a few moments crews for ten cars volunteered, and this speaks volumes for the enterprise and intrepidity of these red-blooded folks of the West. After a day's delay to get ready we started out. It was ten days before a national election and all these men expected to be back in their home city to vote for President. After surmounting almost inconceivable difficulties, at times carrying cars bodily across deep ravines or across flooded rivers and battling with sticky adobe mud caused by two day's rain, besides having serious breakdowns of almost every one of the eleven cars, we finally reached the town of Price.

A few miles beyond this place lies Price Canyon, through which a road once passed, but now the D. & R. G. Railroad occupied the former bed of the road, and, as no other trail had been constructed through the canyon over the sixteen miles from Helper to Colton, it was necessary for the cars to travel around through an exceedingly rough country nearly sixty miles to reach from one of these stations to the other. As I wanted the route located through Price Canyon, arrangements were made to furnish me with a guide for hiking through while the cars made the long trip around.

This guide was a sorry specimen of humanity who, as a hanger-on at the town saloons, had through dissipation become so weakened that by the time we had gone some nine or ten miles of the sixteen, was about played out from the exertions necessary to get over the rough sides of the steep canyon. Here he sat down on a boulder and entreated me to leave him to his fate, as he had all his days been a worthless good-for-nothing and deserved no better end, and, anyway, did not care but would just as soon pass in his checks now as later. In other words, he had not only lost his stamina but his courage, and was willing to give up.

After considerable persuasion and coaxing he, however, consented to make further efforts, and, with a little assistance now and then, managed to make, in a slow and stumbling way, another few miles. Unfortunately we had here a rather gruesome experience. We saw a decomposed body hanging from a tree, evidently of some unfortunate who in despair had committed suicide. This entirely unnerved my companion, and shortly beyond the place where we had passed the hanging man, swaying back and forth in the wind, he refused entirely to make any further efforts, and no coaxing nor even threats had any effect on him. He simply sat down on the ground and refused to rise or pull himself together.

Of course I could not leave the poor wretch there, as it was turning dark and he was too poorly clad to stand the cold of the night in his alcohol-soaked condition. There was nothing else to do but try to carry or drag him along, and this I undertook to do. While he was a man of slight physique, he began to weigh very heavily after we had proceeded a short distance in this manner, especially as I also am not of very heavy frame, and I was compelled to make frequent stops for rest. The last mile into Colton I was no longer able to carry him, but dragged him along, a few feet at a time, between stops for breath.

When we finally reached the steps of the little frame building which constituted the hotel, I was almost as near in as my burden, but the sight of the cars parked around the building cheered me up wonderfully. I found my company of scouts discussing plans to enter the canyon on a search for us as I opened the door and entered the hotel office. Unfortunately the little town was dry. I say unfortunately, because in this case the specific needed for my guide was a generous dose of his accustomed stimulant more than any other remedy. After searching the town over we finally unearthed a small bottle of whiskey, and when a tumblerful of the raw poison was forced down his throat he began to give signs of life. In an hour's time he seemed as good as new and with a more rosy view on life—in fact, was not at all disposed toward quitting this mundane sphere just then nor in the near future.

When our party eventually reached Salt Lake City we had spent twelve days covering the three hundred miles from Grand Junction, and it was with genuine regret that I parted with those fine fellows, "the boys of 1912."

I had the satisfaction within a year to pilot my car over a new highway through Price Canyon, located on the route over which I had made the preliminary investigation, and on that trip I traveled from Grand Junction to Salt Lake City in two days, an evidence of the work which had been done during the year to eliminate the worst places on this entire route.

Pan, My Pal

Pan is a blue-blooded aristocrat with a family tree as old and a pedigree as unblemished as the proudest and highest in the "tight little island" where Burke's peerage is the main guide to "Who is Who." His ancestors had carried their blue ribbons and bow knots as proudly as any duke his crown and ermine cloak. Besides, no ermine cloak could be more white and flawless than the white coat which Pan wears. Unlike many a scion of nobility, Pan is true as steel and the best friend a man could ever have, his unselfishness and devotion are something beautiful and inspiring and his faithfulness beyond doubt. Pan is a "regular fellow," smart, active and ever alert.

Pan is a wire-haired fox terrier from the Sabine Kennels, down in Texas. His sire was transplanted to the banks of the Sabine from England, after having won pre-eminent honors at the most important bench shows, but now when he wistfully looks towards the East with homesick longings he only sees the Louisiana shore on the other side of the river. Pan is a twin; his brother is called Peter, and the pair were named thus in honor of Maud Adams, who undoubtedly never knew of their existence, and thus missed a real pleasure.

When I first saw Pan he was romping around in a grass-carpeted, wire-netted enclosure with nearly two hundred playfellows, and a wonderfully bright and lively picture they made. It was my task that morning to choose from among this kaleidoscopic jumble of jumping scampering young dog flesh an individual which appealed to me the strongest as most likely to become a boon companion and real comrade on the road. A kindly fairy guided my judgment and Pan became our pal on many a transcontinental motor hike. He shares with us the good and the bad, is patient and wise, always sleeps with one eye open and ear ever cocked, is an apt scholar, proud of what he has learned, and never did anything deserving chastisement but one—and then he escaped it.

The first day on the road Pan suffered intensely from sea-sickness, or rather car-sickness, and refused to be comforted and coddled. In all his six months of existence he had had no such experience, and he looked at us reproachfully and miserably with his pleading eyes. However, in a couple of days he began to take interest in his fellow passenger and to notice his swiftly changing surroundings. In a week he acted like a seasoned globe trotter, developed an enormous appetite and soon began, as we pulled up at a hotel entrance for a night stop, to look at the hostelry with a speculative eye, trying to figure out in advance if any objection would be offered to his sharing our room with us. We became so fond of the cute little runt that when some landlord, after reasonable pleadings, remained adamant in his objections to dogs, we would seek some other hotel or even go to some other town rather than leave our tiny friend alone in the garage for the night.

When Pan was a little over a year old he had traveled far and wide and became as car wise as an insurance adjuster. At this time we again happened to visit his native State. Somewhere near the edge of the Staked Plain, in the Panhandle, some good-roads enthusiasts presented our driver with a pair of young opossums, which he kept in the pocket of one of the front doors of the car, unknown to me. The little things were only some five inches long, exclusive of their prehensile tails, and were quite tame. Pan's continuous interest in that corner of the car aroused my curiosity and I soon, of course, discovered the cause. The black, bead-like eyes and pig-like snouts of the little pets did not appeal to our party, but as the driver promised to ship them to his home when we reached Colorado, we raised no objection to carrying them that far. Not so Pan; he had to be continually restrained from making a raid on that door pocket.

At Colorado Springs we were the guests of some friends, and here of course Pan had to make the best of his quarters in the stable. In the garage, next door to the stable, the opossums were kept in a box placed on a shelf. The next morning after our arrival the driver announced the disappearance of his pets. He had found the slats covering the box slightly displace and the opossums gone. A rigid search of the premises failed to discover their whereabouts, but I noticed that Pan tried somewhat ostentatiously to look unconcerned—in fact, so much so that my suspicion was aroused.

As we started to leave the stable, apparently satisfied that the 'possums were not there, I seemed to note a smug look of satisfaction on Pan's face and determined to return shortly. After a lapse of an hour I came back stealthily and, upon jerking the door suddenly open, found the little rascal playing with a 'possum tail as a kitten with a ball of twine. He knew that he had been caught red-handed and ran to a corner, whining for mercy. That was the time he deserved corporal punishment but didn't get it. It was not in my heart to give him anything stronger than a round scolding in appreciation of his cunning in hiding the remains of his victims from our view when we first inspected the stable. The 'possums had escaped from their box and, prowling around, had gone through a drain into the stable and here met their end.

As I am writing this, Pan, now a staid world-wise dog, with the experience of four years of roaming over the highways of the country showing in his wise, kind eyes, sits at my feet and is probably wondering what I am writing about. I can wish my friends nothing better than the good fortune to acquire a pal like Pan.

Close Connection

Between Salt Lake City, Utah, and Ely, Nevada, the Lincoln Highway and the Midland trail, now the Roosevelt National Highway, coincide for about three hundred miles. The country between these two cities is most bleak and forbidding, albeit that it has, like all desert regions, a certain fascination of its own. The Great Salt Lake Desert, formerly called the Great American Desert and the Sevier Desert, besides several desert mountain ranges between the two cities, made it a matter of great concern to locate the route not where the best but the least bad condition prevailed. In hunting for this least bad route I traveled all the possible options available north and south of the lake, and am probably the only man who has covered them all.

While the route as now located has been so far improved as not only to rob it of any possible danger but even make traveling over it a matter of merely covering ground and enjoying the opportunity to view this arid section without worry or apprehension, it was entirely another matter to roam through this region in a motor car while searching for the line of least resistance for a highway, water begin the constant anxiety of our party.

On one of these trips we went south from Ely via Newhouse to Milford, Utah, and made this little town without serious hardships. From Milford our route lay northeast across a corner of the Sevier Desert, and we learned that there was no water for about forty-five miles. As a strong wind blew from the southwest, thus compelling us to travel with it, we were somewhat apprehensive in regard to having our motor overheat, and consequently loaded our car with extra water containers, so that on starting out we carried an extra supply of twelve gallons of water for our radiator, surely enough, as we thought, to cover all contingencies. My wife, the mechanic and I made up the party of three.

We had not gone far from Milford, traveling in a cloud of our own dust carried on the breeze at about the same speed as our own, when our motor ran hot. With only slight concern we stopped and filled the radiator. After a while we had to stop and repeat this performance every little while, and eventually, some thirty miles out, our extra water supply ran so low that I realized we would only have enough for possibly another five miles, and that would be ten miles short of the place where we had been told we would find water. In fact, it might be further than ten miles, as the estimate of distances in those days, when motor cars were rare, often was a matter of mere guesswork.

Before we had covered even the five miles we were entirely out of water and the engine was boiling hot. We were compelled to stop. From a nearby knoll I surveyed the entire surrounding country. There was nothing in sight but sandy wastes with black lava hills jutting out here and there. Things looked indeed gloomy, as being stalled in that arid country, waterless, was really more than serious.

My wife, who from long experience in roughing it never loses heart, then hit upon a bright idea. In a box in the tonneau we had six bottles of carefully packed and much treasured claret of a choice vintage, made and presented to us by a friend in California who owned a fine vineyard. Friend wife generously offered to sacrifice the wine and accordingly the box was opened and the contents of the bottles poured into the radiator, which was hardly more thirsty than ourselves. Nevertheless, we refrained from sharing even a tiny drop without motor, which took it all and could have used more when the last bottle was emptied.

With new heart we cranked up and proceeded, the motor doing very well on its unaccustomed diet. However, in a couple of miles we were again compelled to stop from the same old cause, and we were now without further resources. About a hundred yards ahead was a slight elevation, and in order to take another look around—which, however, I felt in my heart would be entirely useless, I climbed up the slight grade, and to my utter astonishment there appeared less than another hundred feet away—a pool of water.

I rubbed my eyes and looked again, to make sure it was not one of those cruel desert mirages. But no, there it was. True, it was murky and dark green, but it was water, really wet water. It seemed too good to be believed all at once. The liquid was unfit to drink, and though we suffered keenly from thirst we were compelled to confine ourselves to filling radiator and the extra containers. Some twelve miles further and we were out of the desert and among cedar-grown hills, and here we found the ranch house of a Mormon, where a bubbling spring of cool water made us all forget the past danger of the day. The ranchman, about whose house some dozen children of very nearly the same age were playing and staring at us with a curiosity indicating the rarity of visits from people of the outside, assured us that he had never known water to remain for any length of time in any of the many depressions of the lava-strewn region where we found it, and assured us there had been no rain in the region for months. Yet we found it.

Road conditions in the mountains, illustrated below at Granite Mountain in Tooele County, UT, were particularly difficult. Early cars were ill-equipped to handle the high elevation. (University of Michigan)

Deadly Figures

Next to being asked what tires I use and can recommend, the question probably most often put to me is how many miles I have traveled in my many years of pathfinding. My answer is invariably that I do not know, though I have most likely traveled more different (note the different) miles on rubber tires than any man in the world. This I believe to be true.

When anyone makes an offhand statement that he has traveled two or three or four or even five hundred thousand miles, he should not be taken too seriously. Just apply the yardstick to these figures and note how they dwindle. I noted in the press only recently that a comparatively young man had traveled about eight hundred thousand miles in fifteen years and that he hoped to cover a round million, or a distance equal to forty times around the earth at the equator.

Let us stop for a moment and analyze these figures. Eight hundred thousand miles in fifteen years makes fifty-three thousand three hundred and thirty-three miles a year, or over one hundred and forty-one miles a day for every day in the year—Sunday, holiday and weekday. If a day should be missed it would be necessary to double up the next day or to cover over two hundred and eighty-two miles. To do this summer and winter, rain or shine, mud or snow, for fifteen consecutive years is, of course, preposterous. That anyone has covered one-half that distance in that time is not impossible, but hardly within the range of probability.

I confine myself to the safe statement that I have made more motor trips across the United States, East and West, North and South, than any other man, and that these trips were mostly over different routes.

The Black River Crossing

On the "Trail-to-Sunset"—later called the Apache Trail because it leads through the Apache Indian Reservation and connects Springerville, Arizona, and the National Old Trails route with Phoenix via Fort Apache, Globe and Roosevelt Dam—the Black River separates the White Mountains from the Natanes Range.

When I arrived at Fort Apache, in the spring of 1911, with the first transcontinental truck and its crew, after spending eight days covering forty-two miles across the White Mountain plateau, we were all of us about ready for a rest. In discussing the trail across the Black River, some twenty miles south of the army post, with the commanding officer, I learned that the river was at flood stage and that three army wagons and a company of soldiers, returning from the Mexican border, had been in camp on the other side of the river for a week waiting for the water to subside in order to be able to ford across.

As I had crossed at this place the previous fall and was acquainted with the lay of the land at the crossing and also because I felt that I knew what my crew could accomplish with the truck, I made the proposition to the commanding officer that if he would furnish me with a troop of cavalry, twenty strong, I would guarantee to get his army wagons across after having crossed with the truck. He readily accepted my proposition and next morning I learned that the troop had started out at daylight and would be at the crossing when we arrived.

The trail leads through a very rough and broken country, the former stronghold of the notorious chief Geronimo and his band of murderous Apaches, where plenty remote and secure hiding places abounded. Our progress over the twisting, uneven and often steep trail was naturally slow and it was the middle of the afternoon before we arrived at the river, where we found the cavalry encamped.

The Black River is a swift mountain stream and only some seventy-five feet wide. Upon looking on the racing, leaping and dancing current I confess that I felt somewhat uncertain that we would be able to make our words good. However, the officer of the post like a good sportsman had called my bluff, though when made it was not intended as such, so there was nothing to do but make the attempt. The truck was a seven-ton affair, as big as a furniture van, and was heavily loaded, hence I scarcely feared that it would be swept off its feet—or rather wheels. But it was difficult to gauge the depth of the stream on account of the swift current, and besides I knew that several large boulders were in the river-bed, and these of course could not be seen for the same reason.

One of the cavalrymen volunteered to cross with a thin clothesline, swimming his horse across. The animal was instantly swept off its feet and landed on the opposite shore more than five hundred feet downstream. After coming up to a point opposite the truck the trooper attempted with help of the soldiers at the army wagons to pull a heavy rope with block and tackle arrangement across. The raging current, getting a good hold of the four strands of rope, threatened to pull the entire crew into the water before it was pulled half way across. The spray spouted many feet in the air when the current struck the rope.

A pair of army mules were hitched to the thin line, which in addition was run around a nearby tree. This accomplished the end desire and the block and tackle was made fast to a big tree. Four mules were hitched on and slowly the big truck nosed its way into the water. Gradually, inch by inch, it crept across, luckily missing the boulders, though it partly climbed one of them and slid off. These were anxious moments. When the vehicle had reached midstream the top of the radiator was barely visible above the water. The magneto and carburetor had, of course, been removed.

Upon nearing the far bank the ascent was quite steep and the water deepest. The mules pulled their best with every ounce of strength on the hames, the rope creaked and groaned and every man held his breath. When finally the truck stood on the other bank, high and dry, the crossing accomplished successfully, there was a release of pent-up feelings and a lusty cheer issued from every throat. As for myself it was a moment of supreme satisfaction, this successfully having accomplished something which had been supposed to be undoable.

But the rub was that I was still on the wrong side of the river, as I had remained to take photographs of the task in hand. There was nothing else to do but emulate the trooper who had swum his horse across. Bidding a hearty goodby to the company and mounting one of the horses, I plunged in with a camera held high above my head in each hand. The well-trained horse seemed to know just what was expected of him and pluckily fought the grasping current, while I had quite a job to stay on with the water up to my waist at times and both arms high in the air.

When the other bank was safely attained there remained yet the task of getting the army wagons across. This was accomplished by loading them heavily with boulders and reversing the operation used with the truck, while the soldiers swam the mules across. Just as night fell the work was done. We went into camp where the soldiers had been encamped so long and the campfire of the troops soon lighted up the opposite shore. By daybreak the bugle sounded and with shouts of godspeed we parted company in opposite directions.

Today there is a bridge at this crossing, but almost every spring flood of this turbulent stream causes serious damage to it and entails extensive repairs. At least two bridges have been swept away by the flood from this location.

Just Frogs

At one time, while traveling over what was later named the George Washington Highway in South Dakota, I encountered a most curious phenomenon. I had heard that once in a blue moon such incidents happened in various sections of the prairie states, but had never before, nor have I since, experienced anything like it.

As we motored along a natural prairie road an immense black cloud was racing fast towards us, portending one of those cloudbursts which so often visit the prairie country at any uncertain time during the hot summer months. On meeting the blast of cold wind which indicated that the downpour might start any moment, we hastened to get out the curtains and fasten them on the car. But as almost everyone who has had occasion to do a similar stunt in a jiffy will know, the right curtains got in the wrong place and vice versa, so that by the time we had them properly sorted and really were on the way to do the thing right, the storm struck us.

We had to abandon the effort and hopped into the car to get under cover. Here we huddled, holding the curtains before us shields against the fierce slanting rain which literally fell in sheets while flashes of lightning played about us continuously. These sudden storms on the open prairie are no jokes, and as no one knows where lightning may strike we certainly spent an anxious fifteen minutes.

Shortly the storm had passed over. Our cover had been insufficient and in spite of our attempts to protect ourselves we were wet as drowned rats. The whole inside of the car was also wet and full of hopping, wriggling little black things which gave us all a creepy feeling. They proved to be tiny frogs about the size of a man's thumbnail. In a few minutes the sun appeared and we saw the road ahead and the ground in all directions just black with little frogs, which jumped, lively and frisky, in all directions. There were millions upon millions of them. It was impossible to set a foot down without crushing dozens of the creatures.

After putting on skid chains we proceeded slowly and for five miles saw frogs as far as the eye could see in all directions. Then all at once we were out of this area of animate things and it felt almost like reaching shore after a voyage through turbulent seas. For every revolution of the wheels our tires crushed hundreds of frogs and we must have killed millions of them before reaching what may be termed dry ground.

The theory of local people who have seen similar phenomena is that these frogs are sucked up out of a swampy region by a waterspout and carried a great distance, possibly a hundred or more miles before some atmospheric condition is encountered which causes the precipitation. It certainly was an eerie experience.

The New York Times published this illustration in 1913 of the two trails charted west. The pathfinding effort was largely due to Westgard's efforts.

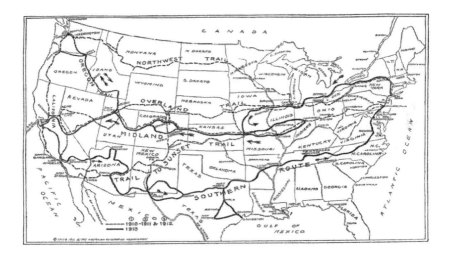

Diamondbacks

Having motored into so many remote regions, far from habitations, in all of our Western, Southwestern and Southern States, I have seen thousands of rattlesnakes of many different varieties, from the almost black swamp rattler of Florida to the small sidewinder of the Colorado desert, in California; from the green rattler of the Staked Plains to the pale, dusty specimen of western Kansas, and the vicious kind in the Rio Grande Valley of New Mexico; even the rock "varmint" of Nevada and the kind that the Hopi Indians—who seemingly are immune against their poison—carry in their mouths during the weird snake dances. But, in my opinion, the Texas diamondback rattlesnake, found in the mesquite chaparral along the lower reaches of the Rio Grande Valley, takes first prize both for size and general cussed viciousness.

At one time while I was traveling a few miles back from the Rio Grande, going from Eagle Pass to La Pryor, we were following a lonely trail through the chaparral when, on account of the sand and general heavy condition of the going, dusk overtook us while we were yet many miles from our destination for the night. It was an unusually mild evening, following the first really warm day of the early spring. We had seen no snakes at all during many days of travel in that country and assumed that they were still hibernating. As the day was waning we saw our first snake and thought nothing of it. Shortly we ran across another in the middle of the trail, and from then on for the next hour saw more rattlesnakes than we ever had in all our lifetime before. They all seemed to be in the trail, and we drove over and crushed several hundreds of them. They all were of unusually great size, full-grown specimens, and evidently had all emerged from their winter quarters at the same time, called forth by the warm spring day.

One particular chap was of such great size that I stepped out of the car to kill him for his skin. He retreated to a small bush near the edge of the trail and fought back fiercely, making repeated strikes at the heavy stick with which I belabored him. It was my intention to injure his skin as little as possible, and it took some time to dispatch him, as he seemed to have more than the nine lives traditionally allotted to the cat. However, he finally had to give up, and I slung him on the running board while his jaws were yet spasmodically making their plucky, dying attempts to open and strike.

Next morning I had a Mexican skin him. This was done by cutting off his head and tail and turning his skin inside out, peeling it off the carcass. The skin was then reversed, the tail end tied with a string, and the snake's beautifully marked cover filled with cornmeal to absorb all the moisture from its inside. Finally, the head opening was tied securely with a string, and the affair, looking like a huge sausage, was thrown across some of the baggage in the tonneau. I noticed the Mexican carefully buried the broad, arrow-shaped head of the snake in order to remove the danger of anyone stepping on it and possibly being poisoned by its fangs.

When we pulled up to the door of one of the hotels in San Antonio, one of the negro bellhops solicitously came out to help remove the baggage. His eyes fairly bulged and his complexion turned almost pale with fright when he reached in for the suitcases and his hand came in contact with the filled snakeskin. With a howl he jumped back and no argument could induce him to again approach the car until I had removed the "snake." To tell the truth, this descendant of the tempter of the Garden of Eden did look mighty lifelike until one noticed the absence of its terminal extremities.

It was a real Texas diamondback, the pattern on its back being most clearly marked in black, gray and white, a really rattling big rattler.

The Top of the Cascades

For some years after the advent of the automobile the State of Washington, as far as concerned motor vehicle traffic, was to all practical purposes almost like two different hemispheres. The great "Inland Empire," as the East Washingtonians proudly, and with justice, like to call their part of the State, was practically isolated from the Puget Sound counties by the Cascade range of mountains, except for a rough trail with steep grades through the dense forest which clad Snoqualmie Pass. This corduroyed and slab-lumbered trail was in fact so exceedingly difficult to negotiate and its passage attended with such hazards and strain on the heavy, low-powered motor cars of that day that the motorists who crossed the range in a season could almost be counted on the fingers of one hand. In addition to the difficulty of the pass, the necessity of ferrying five miles along the shores of Lake Ketchelus was another deterrent, as the ferry service, intended for the limited horse-drawn traffic which found its way over this route, was very primitive and uncertain.

This was the condition when I laid out what I called the Northwest Trail from Chicago to Seattle, which route is now called the National Parks Highway, because it gives access by short side trips from the main trunk line to three national parks—the Yellowstone, Glacier and Mount Rainier. After plowing through deep dust, a sort of volcanic ash, in Central Washington, crossing the apple belt of the Columbia River country, and making the passage over Blewett Pass, the first car to accomplish this feat—and it was some difficult task, with the steep grades and many unbridged boulder-strewn crossings of Peshastin Creek—we finally arrived at the shores of Lake Ketchelus.

We rang the bell which was placed here to call the ferry from its "home port," some five miles distant, the sound being perfectly audible even that far away in this silent solitude, and, in fact, much intensified by the echo which was thrown back as from a sounding-board by the forest-clad, steep shores. After nearly two hours' wait we managed with great care to embark the car on the none too safe-appearing old scow which, in connection with a tiny gasoline-motored launch, constituted the ferry. This ferry, by the way, was made unnecessary the following year by reason of the construction of a highway along the shore of the lake. On disembarking we set out at once up the trail towards the summit of the Cascades, which like saw-teeth pierced the sky ahead of us. The ascent was fairly gradual, with occasional steep pitches, but the trail itself was exceedingly rough and narrow, winding in and out among giant pines and firs.

In the middle of one of these steep places we encountered an old man who was endeavoring to coax an emaciated old horse to exert another ounce of effort in attempting to drag a dilapidated buggy up the trail. The bony structure of the horse was so evident under its gray, mangy skin that he appeared more like a skeleton of a horse than one of the flesh and blood. The buggy was held together with generous applications and sundry bandages of baling wire. All in all, the whole outfit—man, horse and buggy—was about as nearly played out as any outfit I had ever seen in all my travels.

As neither kicks, curses nor kind words seemed to have any effect on the poor brute in the shafts, and as it was impossible in that particular spot to drive around this archaic assembly, we stopped the car and offered to help. Putting shoulders to the wheels, we pushed the buggy as well as the horse along for a couple of feet, when the worn equine, evidently thinking it was time for a real siesta, or possibly figuring that we might carry him as well as the buggy to the top of the grade, lay down in the shafts with a thud, breaking at the same time one of the shafts and the single-tree. Unhitching the ropes, which served for harness, and backing the buggy, we fixed up the damage with wire, with which the buggy was principally loaded, and then tried to induce the horse to realize that it was entirely unethical to slumber in the middle of the trail, at least out of hours. But he refused to understand our various arguments, unconcernedly stretching out on his side and continuing his visit to horse heaven, the old gentleman in the meantime insisting that his faithful friend was neither balky nor worn out-no, sir, no more than he was himself—but merely a little tired. And when he became tired, he usually took a rest.

As the old man's appearance seemed to point to an age of close to four score years, and conveyed no indication of prosperity or means of feeding either himself or his horse, this assurance was not very encouraging. However, his story proved interesting, as he told of his having traveled all the way from Texas with his outfit; had spent seven months on the trail and was headed for Canada, where he had heard there were fine chances to get free land and opportunities were offered to "get ahead" for anyone that was strong and willing to work. He presented such an illuminating example of optimism and undiluted pluck that we forced to gaze at the man in wonder and admiration.

Meanwhile, the horse had evidently figured out that there was nothing further to be gained by playing 'possum so he struggled to his feet and started wobbling ahead, and we wisely let him go to get him out of the way. Hauling and pushing the buggy to the top, we found him calmly waiting to be again tied to the shafts. He positively seemed to enjoy the support of the two wooden braces, as they furnished him something to lean on. With a generous donation from our commissary, we left the old gentleman and his horse with the best wishes for a successful ending of his adventure. I can almost assert that I saw the old joker of a horse slyly wink at me as I turned in the car to wave a final greeting to his master as we forged ahead. How on earth this outfit negotiated the grades that we found farther up the trail has always been a mystery to me.

After battling with the rotten corduroy road, which by reason of the fact that the sun never penetrated through the dense tops of the immense forest trees was everywhere slippery and slimy, we eventually found good going at North Bend and arrived at Seattle safely. The photographs which I had taken to show the condition of this sole route for vehicle connection between the east and west part of the state was so convincing, when reproduced in the Seattle papers, accompanied by a story of the state of affairs and the importance of having them remedied, that a movement was set on foot to effect necessary improvements. Two years subsequently an $800,000 highway with easy grades throughout carried the increasing motor-car traffic through Snoqualmie Pass. This year and next, 1920 and 1921, the highway will be paved with concrete.

In the Bighorns

Some years ago I made a survey of the Black and Yellow Trail, which is a direct cross-country route from Minneapolis to the Yellowstone National Park, and gets its name because it runs through the Black Hills of South Dakota and Yellowstone Park. It crosses the northern part of Wyoming and in this region traverses a rough and unsettled country, running across a region of so-called "bad lands," besides crossing the Bighorn mountains and the Powder and Bighorn rivers.

We traveled with two cars, a large one for carrying passengers and their personal baggage, and a small, light car to carry tents and general camp equipment. We encountered considerable rough going in South Dakota, at one time passing through a large section where dry farming had been attempted by many settlers who had been induced by unscrupulous land agents to buy land at low rates and on long payments, only to be compelled to give up the hopeless task of raising crops after several years of deprivation and hardships. They had simply left for other parts, abandoning their equity in the lands and all improvements. Their abandoned dugouts or small shacks dotted this region and remained as monuments to their brave efforts and blasted ambitions to be self-supporting and produced owners of homes. These were indeed monuments of sadness, failure and despair.

Near Huron we passed a large ranch owned by a half-breed Indian, on which he raised buffaloes. The American bison, even those kept on fenced ranches, had become so scarce since their extermination as wild game, that specimens were in much demand for zoological gardens all over the country, and this particular herd had so dwindled that their owner desired to dispose of those remaining, some fifty animals. They were offered to the United States Government, but, through parsimony, red tape, or lack of foresight, or possibly a mixture of all three, the negotiations were so prolonged that the owner of the herd accepted an offer for them from the Canadian Government, and these splendid, slow-breeding animals were thus lost to our country.

Leaving Deadwood, in the Black Hills, where the surrounding rich mining region has much besides the tales of the exploits of Deadwood Dick and the experiences of the Deadwood stage to make it famous, we traveled via the poetically named town of Sundance, reminiscent of Indian ceremonies, and across the "bad lands," a region where nothing but sage brush grows—and often not even that—to Buffalo, and then entered the Bighorn mountains after descending the steep grade of Crazy Woman's Hill, on the creek of the same euphonious name.

Everything went well and we expected to reach Ten Sleep—another illuminating Indian name, one sleep meaning a day's travel—by night. As the trail was very dim we hesitated at one place, where it forked and either trail showed about the same usage, or rather lack of usage; and, as most often is the case, he who hesitates is lost. Thus we chose the wrong fork, and after ascending and descending several steep moraines which tested our cars to the utmost, we finally attained the crest of the mountains, where my aneroid showed an altitude of 9,500 feet. It was now near dusk and I realized we had taken the wrong fork, some fifteen miles back. To make matters worse, as we were struggling out of a small swampy spot the strain became too great for metal to stand and our rear live axle snapped.

Here was a cheerful situation: forty miles from the nearest habitation, which was at Ten Sleep; nearly two miles up in the air, and, to cap the climax, a very slender supply in our commissary box. Although it was practically midsummer, only barely past the middle of August, the evening and night was bitterly cold and the blazing logs of the campfire felt very grateful. Realizing that we would be out of food in another twenty-four hours, I was mighty glad that we had two cars with us. Next morning the small car was dispatched to Ten Sleep to have the broken axle welded, if perchance there was a blacksmith in the little town; if not, it would have to proceed to Worland, another forty miles beyond and rough going all the way. In either case it would be gone at least two days, so that the prospects of reduced rations for the remaining party loomed bright indeed.

Strolling around the neighborhood of the camp during the day, it seemed to me on a couple of occasions that I heard the distant bleating of sheep, but again, on listening intently for a repetition of the sound, I was unable to verify my impression. The next morning, after a slim breakfast, we had an empty foodbox—and our appetites were mighty keen up there in the wonderfully pure air. Again I thought I heard sheep bleating, and determined to set out on a trip of exploration. After going a couple of miles I knew that I had chanced upon the right direction, and that my impression about the sheep was right, for now I very distinctly heard the sheep and also the barking of the dog.

Hastening in the direction of the sound, I found a flock of some two thousand sheep, with a herder in attendance. After an explanation of our predicament, he directed me to his wagon, his lonely home on wheels, and told me to help myself from his ample commissary, containing flour, bacon, condensed milk, canned fruit and other necessaries. He also lent me his horse to carry the stuff to our camp, but could not leave his flock for fear of it being attacked by wolves. This generous hospitality put us beyond danger of privation. On returning with the horse later in the day, the herder refused absolutely to accept my recompense for the food and would only take some magazines which I had brought him.

That night the other car returned from Ten Sleep, where the axle had been welded by a blacksmith, who fortunately was located there, and also bringing a supply of food. Next morning we set out retracing our way towards the fork where we had made our mistake three days before. Before reaching that far, however, the axle once more broke in the same place, and again the little car had to make the rough journey to Ten Sleep in another effort to have the damage repaired. That night a heavy snow fell on the mountains, and it was bitterly cold. While wood was plentiful it was wet from the snow, and thus it was difficult to keep the campfire ablaze, causing us keen suffering, as we had hardly sufficient clothing to keep warm under such conditions after dividing it with two of our party who were quite thinly clad.

Another two days and our little savior car appeared, and once more we were able to move. This time we made within twenty miles of Ten Sleep when for the third time the axle snapped, again in the same place.

The little car's journey to the blacksmith shop and return this time was made within twenty-four hours, and eventually we reached the little town and, to our great delight, found as clean and well kept a little hotel as it had ever been our pleasure to encounter. For many a long day the comforts of this place, with its good home-cooked food, remained in our grateful memory, after the trials and tribulations on top of the Bighorns.

Two early 20th Century motorists show that the snow drifts in the far West could prove difficult. (University of Michigan)

Photographing the Red Man

It is said that all Indians are averse to being photographed. My pathfinding has at one time or another brought me in contact with most of our Indian tribes, and as I am a consistent camera fiend my experiences have shown that upon the whole this assertion is fairly correct. However, with few exceptions I have found that the Indian is generally a shrewd enough business man to appear hostile towards the camera until he is properly mollified by a dose of palm oil. The more copious the dose the more amenable towards the ordeal he becomes and the less fear of "the evil eye" he exhibits, even to the extent of overcoming religious scruples.

On the Flathead reservation, in Montana, I was told that it would be absolutely impossible to get Chief Louis Pierre to pose for a snapshot, but being properly introduced and having applied the universal persuader in a diplomatic and generous manner, he consented to "have his picture took." However, first he sent one of his bucks for his favorite cayuse, as he deemed it below his dignity to be photographed afoot, like the humbler members of his household. Mounted on his horse, he issued commands to his followers and ordered them to procure their rifles and guns from the tepees. He then arranged them to suit his idea of martial position and, taking a stand at the head of the line, grandiloquently signaled to "let her go."

At another place on the same reservation I noticed a tepee picturesquely located near the shore of Flathead Lake and surrounded by small white birch trees. It made such an unusually pleasing picture to the eye that I jumped out of the car and approached, in the meantime adjusting the focus as well as the aperture and speed of the shutter to suit the light. As I snapped the shutter someone on the inside of the tepee heard the click and an Indian came out with a bound, leveling a Winchester rifle at me. He looked fiercely at me and insisted that I take out the film and destroy it in his presence. But again the silver-tongued clink of coin made it all right.

Once, among the Mohave Indians near Needles, California, I attempted in vain to persuade several picturesquely squalid individuals to consent to being photographed. By various ruses I had managed to steal a few snapshots, when I encountered an exceptionally good subject in the way of an old crone, sitting before her reed hut, making pearl watchfobs. I used my most persuasive arguments and bought more than enough watchfobs to last me for the rest of my life; but it was no use, she persistently and most emphatically refused to be photographed. As I had my camera open, with proper adjustments except as to focus, I surreptitiously set this at twenty feet and turned on my heel, ostensibly to leave the neighborhood. When I was about twenty feet away from the hut I suddenly whirled around and snapped the button.

The old squaw showed surprising agility in getting to an erect position. She picked up a couple of stones and hurled one of them with great force directly at me, exhibiting the greatest fury as she came running towards me. Fortunately I dodged the first missile, turned on my heel and beat an ignominious retreat at top speed. My driver had the car nearby with the motor running, and as I jumped in the second stone came whistling through the air and struck the fender of the car, making quite a dent in it. As I turned around to watch the enemy, she was picking up another stone and came running after us, but of course in a few seconds we were beyond range.

The Yuma Indians are even more hostile to the camera than their cousins, the Mohaves. Tourists who stop over from transcontinental trains for a visit in the town of Yuma find that these Indians, men as well as women, are most expert at shielding their faces when encountered on the sidewalks of the town. They always have an eagle eye cocked for cameras and are prone to make trouble when they think that someone has succeeded in taking a snapshot of them.

Realizing the situation, I took a drive out on their reservation and visited some of their farms, but was in every instance unsuccessful in persuading any of the tribe by any means whatsoever to consent to be photographed. Even their chief, Pasquale, who seemed most intelligent, would not have his picture taken on my condition. I had about given up the hope of success when I encountered two squaws at a place where the road was completely hidden from the surrounding country by tall reeds. They were returning to their houses on the reservation from a visit to the town. Stopping the car, I pulled out a handful of silver coin and, after much talk and the promise of a dollar apiece, they consented to let me take a photograph of them, provided I was sure that no one was in sight to see the performance and upon my solemn promise that I would not show the pictures to any one in Yuma. I decided to use the plate camera in place of the Kodak, in order to secure a large photo of them and also to insure perfect focus. There is where I made my mistake. While the tripod was being erected and the formidable camera with its black focusing cloth gotten in readiness, the inherent fear of the thing evidently began to take possession of them and make them exceedingly nervous. I noticed their trepidation and hastened to get everything in shape, not even taking the time to procure a careful and sharp focus. As I squeezed the bulb and they heard the click of the shutter, they turned and ran into the reeds as fast as they could, without waiting for their dollars. This disregard of the money convinced me that their fear was genuine and that I might count myself lucky to have secured this picture, even thought the focus proved to be a little off.

Among the pueblos of New Mexico there is little trouble to get Indians to pose for the camera, as they have long since learned that the operation is as painless as it is profitable and that no evil results follow. But some of these tribes have been badly spoiled and have acquired quite an inflated idea of their value as artistic subjects. Thus at Acoma I was not allowed by the governor of the pueblo to unpack my photographic outfit without first paying a fee of five dollars into the local government treasury.

At Zuni I found little difficulty in getting the governor of that pueblo to act as my official guide and introducer to any member of the tribe whom I might want to photograph, of course for a consideration, both to the guide and to the subjects. But when I tried to get permission to picture the Shalako Dances, one of their most picturesque religious ceremonies, I met a most positive refusal and had to give up the effort to do so.

While the Navahos and Hopis do not like to be subjects for the camera and their women will hide their faces so as not even to be able to see the evil contrivance which takes the pictures, it is usually not very difficult to overcome this aversion if diplomatically handled. However, at religious ceremonies it is exceedingly difficult to secure the assent of the heads of the clans to the taking of photographs. But it has been done. The Apaches, Papagos and Pimas are entirely indifferent to the camera and do not mind it in the least.

Americans All

In traveling through the country districts in many our Western, Central Western and even Southern States, one will frequently strike a country inhabited almost exclusively by emigrants from one particular European nation. It impresses one most forcibly that though these people often cling to their native language and in their homes retain in large measure their former method of living, cooking their food and even to some extent of fashioning their clothes, they strongly maintain that above all they are Americans and with great indignation resent any assertions which tend to impugn their whole-hearted loyalty to the Stars and Stripes.

Of course, we have with us anachronisms like the Louisiana French and the New Mexican Mexicans, a large percentage of whom, in spite of living under our flag for generations, do not speak or even understand the English language. Then there are the numerous Indian tribes, the original Americans, of whom only a certain percentage understand our language or care to learn it. However, the foreign immigrants as a rule do learn our tongue in course of time and at least are ambitious that their children shall attend schools and become Americans, in all respects like the majority of their fellow citizens.

But there are localities in some of the more remote regions where these people sometimes become to some extent isolated, and this condition tends to handicap the fulfillment of their desire for intermingling with English-speaking people and to maintain, with small opportunities for a change, their old-country language and ways. Again, there are a few instances where certain nationals, especially if they arrived on our shores when past middle age, find the acquisition of our language so difficult that, in view of the fact that they live among their old-country folks and hence are not compelled to learn any other tongue, they naturally do not make a very serious effort to do so.

Not long ago, I travelled through Illinois on an inspection tour over the Lincoln Highway and had reached a point only a few miles directly south of Chicago, when we were overtaken by a storm which soon made the dirt road so slippery and the going so heavy that we decided to pitch camp in the first likely spot available. This proved to be a country schoolhouse yard with nice clean grass, wood in the shed and good water at the pump. Directly across the road was a neat cottage occupied by the pastor of a nearby German church.

After snugging up the camp I went across to interview our neighbors, having in mind the acquisition of some fresh eggs and milk. A fine-looking man with about seventy years behind him sat on the enclosed porch, and to him I addressed my introductory remarks, but in reply received only a pleasant smile and a sign to step indoors. Here I met a young woman, who explained to me that her father did not understand English, but that she would be very glad to supply our wants. After a few minutes' conversation with her I learned, to my astonishment, that her father had served the nearby church as its pastor forty-five years. As the necessity for learning English had never been present, he had never seriously tackled the task which he had found so full of difficulties when he first arrived.

At another time in Western Illinois we again had trouble with muddy roads and our engine overheated, necessitating a stop for water at a farm house. The dwelling house and barns were neatly painted and the premises as well kept as a suburban estate. Our driver, who was of Polish descent and quite well acquainted with several Central European languages and dialects, went in and asked an old man on the porch if he could have some water from the well. The answer was a vacant stare which eloquently indicated that the request was not understood, so the driver made the same inquiry in Russian, Polish, German and three or four dialects without better success.

Noticing that he started for the well to get the water without the formality of a permission, I called him back and tackled the job of reaching the old gentleman's intelligence myself. Though he evidently was not of the Latin race, I asked him in French and Spanish without eliciting even a glance of understanding, when all at once it occurred to me to try him in one of the Scandinavian tongues, which really should have been the most obvious to try first, in view of the old man's cast of features. As I was born in Norway, I tried him with Norwegian first and struck the right note with the first touch. A sunny smile lighted up his face as a perfect stream of a Norwegian dialect, used in one of the most remote valleys of the mountainous Land of the Midnight Sun, issued from his lips. He told me he had been at his wit's end trying to make out what we were all talking about. The wonder of it was that he had lived right on that farm for forty-two years. As the county was settled almost exclusively by his countrymen, he had never learned English, though he had been a citizen for a generation and voted regularly at every election.

In Northeastern Colorado I camped one night near a farm in a community of Russians, a very small number of whom could speak English. They were good farmers and cast their votes at all elections. In Wisconsin, Minnesota and the Dakotas are many counties where English is rarely heard except where the younger folks congregate without the elders being present.

Covering the Old Spanish Trail along the Gulf Coast in Louisiana, I once had to make a detour across some marsh lands on account of road construction, and before proceeding very far promptly mired too deep to move either forwards of backwards. Noticing a plantation not far away, I proceeded over to the main building and requested from a man in the yard his assistance and the use of a pair or horses, but had to use French before my request was understood. While he understood my bookish French, it was exceedingly difficult for me to understand his patois, or Louisiana French. His people had lived there for generations but had been too proud to try to learn English, and besides it was not at all necessary to take the trouble to do so, as these people do not travel far from home and the neighbors all understand each other. Que voulez vous?

In New Mexico, we arrived one evening at Rito Quemado, in the remote western part of Socorro County, a hundred miles from a railroad. This little Mexican settlement is on the National Old Trails route and I had on another occasion put up overnight at the house of Anastacio Baca, the storekeeper. None of the Baca family understood a word of English, though New Mexico has been under the Stars and Stripes since 1848. We were made welcome with the open-hearted, proverbial hospitality of the Mexican race. While eating our meal, it was most amusing to watch my wife and senora Baca carry on a conversation without either one understanding a word of the other's language. In spite of this, through some feminine intuition or freemasonry of the sex, they seemed to be able to make each other understand without further difficulties than more or less acrobatic gestures, rolling of the eyes and waving of the arms. At least, so the performance looked to me, who was all the time wondering how a mere ignorant male would have succeeded under similar circumstances.

Another thing is soon noticed by any observant traveler into country districts, and that is that he finds no settlements of Hebrews, Italians, Greeks, Turks or Spaniards. These races seem to prefer congregating in cities, and devote themselves to trades and commerce rather than agriculture. The races that make our real farmers—the backbone of our western agricultural regions, the producers of the fruit of the soil—come from Central and Northern European countries. And, best of all, these races amalgamate and fit themselves most readily into things American. They generally come with intention to stay and do stay for good, become citizens and are proud of the privilege.

As I am writing this the 77th Division, having just returned from France, where it made a most glorious record for itself in the World War, is parading up Fifth Avenue, past my office windows. The division is made up of New York City boys drawn from almost every race on earth. Jews from many lands, Italians, Armenians, Poles, Greeks, Czecho-Slovaks, Jugoslavs, Rumanians, Hungarians, Germans, Scandinavians and many other original ingredients of the melting pot, march by, proud of having served the flag—now Americans all and the sinews of the nation.

Some "Hotels!"

Naturally, I have had a rather unusual opportunity in my ramifying motor trips to sample hotels. I have found that there are more varieties of "hotels" in our country than are embodied in the various names of hotel, hostelry, inn, tavern, café, wirthaus, rathskeller, bodega, kaiserhof, pensionat, and all other European varieties of establishments that cater to looking after a wayfarer, all put together. The term hotel is applied indiscriminately to such establishments as the Commodore in New York and the Blackstone in Chicago, or the Ambassador at Atlantic City, whose vast piles look more like huge office buildings than anything else, all the way down through the chromatic scale to such structure as the shack at Cisco, Utah, which proudly exhibits the sign "hotel" over its door, the sole entrance into a hut built of discarded railroad ties stood on end.

Also, the disposition of some of the lordly beings who superintend the management of some of the gilded palaces are as different from that of the humble bonifaces who in their shirt sleeves come out and with glad hand of hospitality help to carry in your baggage as human nature is given to differ.

On my first trip across the United States in a motor car, we put up at one of the more pretentious hotels in one of the largest Middle West cities, a big, multi-storied building with pretensions to have everything of the very latest in comforts and clock-like management, including a special clerk for each floor. That night a thief entered our suite, chloroformed my wife and me, and carried away all our traveling money, amounting to several hundred dollars, but carefully and studiously refrained from touching any of the jewelry which was openly displayed on the dresser.

When we came out of our narcotic coma and realized what had happened and a search divulged the theft, I of course made a complaint to the manager. He merely calmly asserted that such a thing could not happen in his well-regulated establishment and seemed to think that that assertion would suffice, and that I really was quite presumptuous in insisting that it nevertheless had happened. The situation was something like the Irishman in jail who insisted he really was there, though his lawyer maintained that he could not be jailed for the alleged offense.

This hotel typified the high note at one end of the chromatic scale, while the shack at Cisco typified the other extreme or bass note. Within a dozen miles of the little town of Cisco, of a half dozen houses near the Utah-Colorado line, we had the misfortune to break several teeth in the master gear of the differential on our car, and were compelled to stop and stay where we were while our companion car ran into Cisco for a team of horses. In the course of nearly two days these arrived and hauled us in. When we reached Cisco, tired and worn after our trying experience in this desolate country, we were dismayed to find that the "hotel" was a low structure built of discarded railroad ties stood side by side on end, and naturally so low that we had to stoop upon entering.

Asking the woman, whom I found in the kitchen, if she had a room for us, she said: "Sure: help yourself." Inquiring where the room was, she pointed to a pile of blankets, heaped in a corner of the only other room outside of the culinary department, and told us to take one, spread it out wherever our fancy dictated, and right there was our room and also our bed, for which she made the modest charge of fifty cents, payable in advance. While this was somewhat discouraging, we were pleasantly surprised to sit down to a really good home-cooked meal, which with beds prepared by means of our car's cushions made us feel that lots of folks fared worse than we did that night.

In the hot country of the Mohave, Colorado and Gila river deserts there are other hotels besides the well-managed railroads hotels, such as those of the Harvey system, usually named after one of the Spanish conquistadores or padres. At the smaller desert railroad stations—there being no other settlements in the desert— frequently the "hotel" is what is called a tent-house. This kind of a house is wooden as to the floor and the first four feet from the ground up, while the balance, side and roof, is canvas, and there are no windows except screened openings. They make cool sleeping quarters and are often comfortably furnished.

In the non-English-speaking Mexican towns of New Mexico the "hotel" or posada is usually a low adobe structure, cool, clean and comfortable though primitively furnished. It is said that these adobe houses are the easiest kind to build. As Chas. F. Lummis, the writer, puts it: "One merely flays one's lawn, stands the epidermis on end and roofs it."

Having had experience with unwelcome little brown bedfellows in several hotels in small towns of the Middle West prairie states, I have made it a practice to carefully examine the bedding for sign of vermin, even carrying a small electric pocket torch for the purpose, and on several occasions have endured the indignant protest of the landlord or landlady. But, as I told one especially irate host in one of the smaller Western Nebraska towns, I never could get used to these unbidden guests and didn't proposed to furnish them with free board, hence I should have to insist upon the search. Yes, indeed, there are hotels—and hotels.

Lost—But Recovered

At one time when I covered the route later given the long and awkward name of Pike's Peak Ocean to Ocean National Highway we traveled through a rough and, for long stretches, uninhabited country in Colorado and Utah. We had the misfortune to break a rear axle in the big game country of Northwestern Colorado while attempting, to pull out of a deep and sandy arroyo some twenty miles from the nearest habitation. The driver set out to walk the twenty miles for help. While he was gone the rest of our party were soon out of provisions, but fortunately I discovered smoke some two miles off, and upon investigating, found the camp of a couple of Mexican hunters for wild horses. These provided us with food, so we eventually got away all right. It was interesting to note the superb horsemanship and fleet bunch of horses of these hunters. Indeed, they needed fleet amounts to chase, tire out, and finally lasso or corral the best specimens in the herds of wild horses, as these were also very speedy, but had not the same stamina for endurance as the gentle stock.

At a ranch near the state line we had the experience for the first, only and last time in the entire West of being refused something to eat. Not but what there was plenty of provisions at the ranch, but excuses were made that it really was too much bother to get it for us. However, we were eventually able to coax a pitcher of milk and a few slices of bread from the inhospitable queen who evidently lorded it over the household.

On this trip at a little town in Utah, we found quarters for the night in a rather unprepossessing little "hotel" in a small town. After leaving the place next morning my wife discovered that she had left her rosary, as she supposed, under her pillow, and forgot to remove it on arising in the morning. Some days later, upon again reaching a city, I wrote back to the hotel explaining the result of my wife's forgetfulness and asked that the beads be mailed to my New York office, as my wife prized them highly on account of certain associations connected with them.

When, in course of time, we returned to New York and found no trace of the rosary nor any communication from the hotel people of the little Utah town, it was naturally given up as lost and the incident soon forgotten. However, three years later, a package and letter came from the little town. The package contained the rosary and the letter explained that it has just been found under the mattress of the bed my wife occupied when we stopped there.

Some uncharitably-minded person might make facetious remarks about the length of time between the airings of the beds in this hostelry or utter words to that effect. Three years does seem a mighty extended time for the discovery of the lost article as long as it admittedly was found in the very bed where it was said to be lost but, however, my wife was glad to recover her precious beads and I shall naturally refrain from speculations.

Marking the route of the National Park-to-Park Highway was one of Westgard's expeditions.

The Un-named Pass

It was at the time of laying out the Midland Trail, now the Roosevelt National Highway, that I first crossed Nevada in a southwesterly direction. Between Ely and Tonopah, a distance of nearly two hundred miles, there were only four habitations and the country exceedingly barren, of a desert and volcanic nature. We crossed desert valleys and low mountain ranges all the way, but found the going surprisingly good, the soil being for the most part a disintegrated granite, almost like a fine gravel, and this made the ground firm and practically immune to the washing which the occasional cloud bursts generally cause in adobe soil.

Beyond Tonopah, a productive silver mining camp, and Goldfield, the location of one of the really big producing gold mines of the country, the territory becomes rougher. On the entire distance from Goldfield, Nevada, to Big Pine, California, a matter of a hundred and nineteen miles, there are only three inhabited places, Lida, a small mining camp in Nevada, Oasis, a ranch just across the California line, and Gilbert's Ranch. Shortly beyond the latter we began to ascend the White Mountains range through a picturesque, black-walled canyon, and at the summit found a U.S. geological bench mark showing an altitude of seven thousand, two hundred and seventy-six feet.

The descent from the mountain, on an easy gradient through a winding canyon, presented one of the most beautiful views I have seen in California, and the pass formed one of the most impressive entrances into the Golden State. The vista, as one descended the slope of the mountain, reached across the Owen River valley and straight ahead was shut off by the towering wall of the Sierra Nevadas, with Mount Whitney overtopping all the surrounding high peaks. Mount Whitney is 14,500 feet high and the highest peak within the boundaries of the United States. For a hundred miles up and down the valley one could see this rock wall, rising steeply from the valley floor practically without foothills. The top of the sky-piercing peaks were snow-clad, while the valley was green with growing crops, cottonwoods and willows. Above it all the wondrous colors of a glorious sunset touched the shoulders of the peaks with gold, silver and scarlet, contrasting strongly with the somber shadows of the chasms and canyons which rent the mountain side.

The picture was wonderfully impressive and long lingered in our memories. Near the foot of the pass we were met by a delegation from the town of Bishop, in Owen River valley, who came to bid us welcome to California as pioneers over this route and to tender us the hospitality of their town. This delegation was led by Wisner Gillett Scott, then whom no man in California deserves more honor for untiring, intelligent and withal patient work for the development of good roads in the State, a man who has persistently pointed out the practical as well as esthetic value of California's wonderful attractions within the Sierra Nevada range if properly exploited and put within reasonably comfortable reach of visitors.

I asked this delegation the name of the pass which we had just come through, and to my surprise learned that it had no name either locally or on the State maps.

About a year later I accompanied a caravan of some twenty cars from the East over this route and we were again met by the Bishop delegation this time at Oasis Ranch. When we reached the summit of the pass which had impressed me so much the year before, a stop was made before a neat tablet erected at this spot since my last trip. The legend on the tablet read: "Westgard Pass. Named for A. L. Westgard in recognition of distinguished service rendered Trans-Sierra California." A copy of resolutions passed by the Inyo county commissioners, giving the pass my name, was handed me by the delegation. I must say that I feel most deeply the honor shown me by California in naming the beautiful pass after me.

Our National Parks

Unfortunately, nearly all our national parks are located in the West, in the Rocky Mountain, the Sierra Nevada and Cascade ranges, and thus not easily accessible except at considerable expense to the vastly greater percentage of our population. This, of course, could not be otherwise, on account of the topography of the country, and for this reason it is incumbent on all those citizens who have had the good fortune to enable them to spend the time and money to travel through and enjoy these magnificent wild regions to spread broadcast the glories of the mountains, forests, glaciers, peaks, canyons, lakes, streams, animal life and many natural wonders of these parks in order to incite in their fellow citizens a healthy desire to go and do likewise.

There are eighteen national parks, of which ten are especially noteworthy, and all of which should be seen by every American worthy of the name, before he starts globe-trotting. Most of the famous scenic wonders of other lands would not seem to him so impressive if he were in position to draw comparisons between them and those in the national parks of his own land. There are no glaciers in the Alps surpassing those of Glacier National Park in Montana, there are no geysers in the world even approaching in interest those of Yellowstone National Park. Where on earth is there any chasm even faintly approaching in grandeur the indescribable colorful vastness of the Grand Canyon of Arizona? Mount Rainier National Park in Washington is in a class by itself, and Crater National Park in Oregon is a blue gem like the finest jewel, incomparable to any other scenic spot on earth. And where on the face of this mundane sphere is there a spot with charms equal to those of the Yosemite National Park in California? The oldest living things in the world are the giant redwood trees in the Sequoia, now the Roosevelt National Park, in the Sierra Nevadas of California. The prehistoric ruins of the Mesa Verde National Park in Colorado were probably ancient when the Pharaohs build the Pyramids, and the towering peaks, moraines and glaciers of the Rocky Mountain National Park in Colorado are only a few miles from one of the large cities of the West and easily accessible to millions of our people without undue consumption of time or expenditure of money, while the rainbow colors on cliffs and crags in the newly created Zion National Park in Utah defy an artist's brush.

All of these parks—which of course are not parks in the sense of city parks, but vast rugged regions, often thousands of square miles in extent and teeming with perpetually protected game—are left in the primeval condition of nature and are accessible by motor car. The United States Government, with some niggardliness it is true, has constructed roads and trails through them and provided frequent camping places, with concrete cooking stoves adjacent to fuel and good water, besides granting concessions for hotels, stage lines and other conveniences which are administered under the close supervision of government employees. The National Park Service, a branch of the Interior Department, has shown most conspicuous efficiency in the face of decidedly penurious appropriations from Congress, which, it seems to me, has not yet, as a body, shown sufficient appreciation of the importance of these public vacation grounds with their potential recreative and economic benefits to the nation.

A motor-route map of the United States issued by the American Automobile Association shows the location of all the national parks and the best routes leading to them. I have personally compiled this map from actual observation in covering the main trunk-line routes to the parks, and herewith append a brief outline of the proper routes to use to reach the most important of them:

Rocky Mountain National Park, near Denver, Colorado, is reached from the Lincoln Highway or from the Midland Trail; also from the National Old Trails Road and Pike's Peak Ocean-to-Ocean Highway.

Yellowstone National Park is reached by following the Yellowstone Highway from the Lincoln Highway at Cheyenne, Wyoming; by the National Parks Highway or the Yellowstone Trial form Minneapolis, or via the Black and Yellow Trail; also by route deviating from the Lincoln Highway at Salt Lake City or from Rawlins, Wyoming.

Glacier National Park is reached by the Park-to-Park Highway, deviating from the National Parks Highway and the Yellowstone Trail either at Livingston, Three Forks or at Missoula, Montana.

Rainier National Park is reached only from Tacoma, Washington, on the Pacific Highway.

Crater National Park is reached from Medford, Oregon, on the Pacific Highway, or from Lakeview, Oregon, on the National Defense Highway.

Yosemite National Park is reached from Stockton, California, on the Lincoln and Pacific Highways, and via Tioga Pass from the Roosevelt National Highway (Midland Trail).

Roosevelt National Park, formerly Sequoia, is reached from Fresno, California on the National Old Trails Road and will eventually be accessible from Bishop via the Roosevelt National Highway.

Grand Canyon National Park is reached from Flagstaff or William, Arizona, on the National Old Trails Road.

Mesa Verde National Park is reached from Colorado Springs or Pueblo, Colorado, via the Spanish Trail, or from Gallup, New Mexico, on the National Old Trails Route.

Zion National Park is reached from the Arrowhead Trail, which connects the Lincoln, Pike's Peak Ocean to Ocean and Roosevelt National Highways at Salt Lake City, Utah, with the National Old Trail Road, near Needles, California.

The National Parks Service at Washington, D.C., issues maps and regulations of all these parks and anyone may have them for the asking.

The Forage Stations

During the rush of the "forty-niners" to the California gold fields the route through southern New Mexico and the Gila Valley of Arizona was thronged by caravans from the East eager to reach the fabled El Dorado in the shortest possible time. These individual outfits were supplemented by stage lines in 1857 running all the way from San Antonio, Texas, to San Diego and Los Angeles, even to San Francisco, California. These were prosperous days for the murderous Apache Indian bands, which made travel extremely hazardous through southern Arizona. These pitiless shadows of the trail would lurk behind rocks or lie in wait in canyons and swoop down upon emigrant trains and stages, slaying men, women and children and robbing the trains of anything of value.

The Civil War put a stop to travel along this route and the Apaches then began to raid the scattered settlements of whites. Finally, in 1872, the War Department sent General Crook to Arizona, and this doughty soldier and leader soon put a stop to the outrages. However, every now and then the savages would break bounds and start out on murderous raids, and it was not until 1886 when the last fighting unit of the Apaches under the cruel and vicious Geronimo finally surrendered to General Miles, after a most persistent and strenuous chase of thirteen months in the mountains of Sonora, Mexico, that troubles with the tribe were quelled for good. Fort Apache, an army cavalry post, was established during this period on the White Mountains Apache Indian reservation, the garrison acting as a police force and salutary check on any tendencies to further outbreaks.

This army post is located sixty-one miles from Rice, a station on a branch of the Southern Pacific Railroad, to the south, and about one hundred and ten miles from Holbrook, on the Santa Fe Railroad, to the north. As the post is located in a mountainous region on the White River, practically no agriculture is carried on in the section, and all supplies even horse feed, had to be hauled from the two railroad points above mentioned. A considerable portion of this traffic used the rough trail through a very rugged and broken country to Rice, and in order to provide the freighters with quarters for themselves and feed for their mules two forage stations were established on the route, and the running of these stations was let out by contract to civilians, who undertook to have the stations stocked with food for man and beast.

One of these stations was located near the Black River crossing, twenty-one miles from the post, and the other seventeen miles further away in the Natanes range of mountains. At the time of pioneering in a motor car over the Trail to Sunset, now the Apache Trail, we arrived, after successfully risking the ford across the swift, boulder-strewn Black River, at the first forage station just as darkness fell. The keeper of the station and his wife could hardly believe that an automobile had actually arrived at their front door. In fact, the lady had never seen an automobile, as no motor car had ever before chugged its way into this mountain fastness. We were hospitably welcomed to the very primitive accommodations available. While the good lady was preparing our supper the station keeper showed us a rifle which he had only that day procured from an old Indian who the week previous had killed his wife with it and been apprehended by the soldiers that day near the station.

This story, supplemented by others telling of renegade Indians, bears and mountain lions, made my companions somewhat nervous, as this was an out-of-the-way place where few travelers came. However, our hostess assured them that there was no cause for anxiety, because the dogs of which there were several about the place, would be sure to bark if anything unusual happened or if, anybody approached. Being tired after a strenuous day's work, I fell into a sound sleep as soon as my head struck the pillow, and awoke next morning much refreshed after a fine night's rest. Not so my companions. They were wan, with heavy-lidded eyes, for want of sleep. The dogs had barked continuously all night and the poor fellows had been kept on edge for hours waiting for the expected "unusual" to happen, as per the statement of the station keeper's wife.

The next year, when I again covered this route, I was told of a wanton murder of two businessmen from Globe who had taken possession of the abandoned forage station in the Natanes range while hunting and fishing in that section. During their stay two discharged soldiers from Fort Apache also made their quarters there. During one of their meals the soldiers murdered their companions for their pocket change and arms and started across country for the railroad. Ordinarily their crime might not have been discovered for weeks, but it so happened that another couple of hunters were camped for the night not far away and heard the shots. Upon investigating next morning they found the bodies of the murdered men and hastened to Globe to report the crime. A posse set out and the criminals were eventually caught, and were in the jail at Globe awaiting trial when this story was told us at the White River Agency, near Fort Apache.

Upon reaching the forage station at the Black River crossing, where I had stopped the year before, we found it abandoned, and as there yet remained a couple of hours of daylight we pushed on. Near dusk we arrived at the other forage station, where the murders had occurred the previous week. We took possession, installed our cots and used the stove to cook our meals on, and the table and chairs. It was undeniably somewhat gruesome and eerie to sit in this room so redolent with the recent tragedy. Upon discovering the bullet holes in the thin wooden walls, the topic of conversation naturally dwelt upon the crime, its execution and the sordid motives for it.

However, upon lying down on my cot I went to sleep soundly, but was awakened during the night by a scratching sound which readily enough might, in view of the environments, be termed ghostly by anyone with nerves. I ascribed the cause to rats scampering over the rafters above the paper-covered ceiling of the room, but my two companions on this trip acknowledged that they had cold chills running up their backs from fright.

Forest Fires

I never had either the time or inclination to scale Longs Peak, which towers above all the sublime surrounding mountain apexes, with its majestic summit 14,255 feet above the tides of the ocean and its sheer precipice thousands of feet high, facing the east, in the Rocky Mountain National Park in Colorado. But one summer, while we had pitched our camp on Glacier Creek, in the park, I did undertake a hike to Loch Lake, nestling at the foot of a glacier coming off Taylor Peak. This entailed a walk, scramble and climb of some sixteen miles from an elevation of about nine thousand feet at our camp to some twelve thousand feet at the lake.

The trail at one place passed through a section which some years previously had been burned over by a forest fire, the stark, dead and naked trunks, standing erect, bearing incontestable testimony to the millions of dollars of damage, direct and indirect, which is caused each year to our invaluable forest areas by the sheer ignorance and frequently criminal negligence of builders of camp fires. As growing trees are the most beautiful work of nature, the sight of a forest "burn" leaves at the same time a deep sadness and a hot indignation at the carelessness which, through sheer laziness, selfishness or ignorance, caused this arson of a landscape, destroying in a few hours millions of living wonderful trees that, by its slow processes, nature had taken several centuries to create and which it would take more hundreds of years to replace.

Thousands upon thousands of acres of valuable forests are destroyed by fires annually in the United States, even though of late years the rangers of the many National Forests through eternal vigilance and experience save other thousands of acres from a similar fate. From a crow's nest built in a tall tree on a summit or from the top of an observation tower, a ranger spots the first column of smoke, which, by means of range-finders and compass directions telephoned in to the chief ranger's office from two or more stations, is accurately located. Men with axes and shovels hurry to this location and by the expediency of removing trees which would be in the path of the fire or by shoveling sand or earth in incipient blazes, innumerable small fires are extinguished which, if given a free scope, would have the potentiality of destroying thousands of acres of fine forest.

Enos A. Mills, the author-naturalist of Longs Peak Inn, in the Rocky Mountain National Park, has more eloquently described a forest fire in his book, "The Spell of the Rockies," than perhaps anyone else. To know this quiet and reserved man, with his deep knowledge of growing things and his sublime love for the out-of-doors, which for the Rocky Mountain region parallels that of John Muir for the Sierra Nevadas, is a privilege.

When I drove my car up to his home he was much concerned about my dog Pan, as he feared that the chipmunks about the place would be frightened. These beautiful little rodents were so tame that they would feed out of his hand and crawl over his clothes. The blue jay, which had its nest on the porch, would pay little or no attention to the human beings in near proximity. It is a delight to know Mills; his books, with their strong tang of the glorious outdoors, are like an invigorating tonic to an invalid; his home and surroundings are an inspiration.

I have seen the dispiriting sight of forest burns in many States, from the forests of Maine and the Adirondacks to those of the Rockies, Bitter Roots, Cascades and Sierra Nevadas, and I have for days traveled through a pall of smoke which often was carried hundreds of miles by the wind. From mountain summits I have seen the whirling columns of the thick smoke, at times shot through by leaping flames, but only once have I been in such close proximity to the actual nature tragedy that the heat and ashes became oppressive and almost blinding and the roar of the approaching catastrophe indicated that there was real danger to linger in the region. This was in northern Minnesota.

We were traveling along a rough road through the forest. Occasional clearings with crude cabins testified to the efforts of homesteaders to create producing fields. An oppressive heat had been in evidence for some miles and smoke, which smelled of burnt wood, had come on with the wind and became thicker as we progressed. Approaching a clearing, we met a team coming in our direction at a gallop. In the farm wagon was a homesteader and his family. He pulled up short and admonished us to turn back at once, as a forest fire was coming rapidly in our direction and if the wind should increase in force would drive the sweeping flames with incredible speed.

Without stopping to see if we heeded his advice, he started up his team of horses and had soon disappeared, going at top speed. I hesitated from a time in spite of the thickening smoke and the farmer's advice, thinking that after all we would not be in the path of the fire and to turn back would mean the abandonment of the inspection of a route which I was very anxious to cover. However, when I saw a herd of deer cross the clearing ahead with long, frightened bounds I realized that they were undoubtedly the advance column of an army of all sorts of game and wild animals, whose instincts told them of the approaching danger probably more intelligently than the mere speculations of human beings. With considerable trouble we managed to turn the car around in the narrow road and were soon back-tracking our trail with all the speed the narrow and rough road allowed us to use safely. In three or four miles the smoke had become so thick and the ashes carried on the hot wind so blinding that both seeing and breathing became a matter of considerable difficulty, and shortly we could hear the awful roar of the fire as it leaped forward.

With the throttle in the last notch and the car careening perilously, wobbling over the rough road like a drunken man, we fortunately gained open country and freedom from danger only a short distance ahead of the holocaust. I often shudder to think what would have happened if by some mischance we should have had a puncture or hit a stump in the road, or anything else should have happened to prevent us from maintaining our speed or cause us perforce to stop.

A Close Call

During the pioneer days of motoring in the West, the absence of highway bridges over many of the larger rivers caused many hardships and frequently much added mileage for the motorists who ventured into the more remote regions. Usually fords were available for horse-drawn vehicles, but these were often too deep or with too treacherous bottom to serve motor cars, especially if the water were a little higher than low mark. Thus I have been compelled to cross railroad bridges, bumping my way across on the ties, on several occasions when it was absolutely essential to obtain accurate distance measurements along a projected motor highway and making a long detour to find a better crossing was inexpedient.

In this way I have crossed the Colorado River into California at Needles and at Parker, when there were no highway bridges across this stream its entire length, while now there are two such bridges on the main trunk-line highways, at Needles and at Yuma. I have also crossed railroad bridges across the Rio Grande at San Pedro, New Mexico, and the Little Missouri River at Medora, North Dakota, but the only time that such an adventure entailed a risk and in fact a real danger was when I attempted to cross a railroad bridge over the Powder River near its confluence with the Yellowstone River, in Montana.

At this place there was a ford which ordinarily could have been negotiated with a motor car, but a flood had caused such a rise of the water that an attempt to cross by fording was out of the question.

By making a detour of over fifty miles we could have crossed the stream by a bridge, but that expedient did not appeal to me, so I presented credentials, which I had fortunately provided myself with, to the boss of the railroad section gang from the general superintendent of the railroad. These commanded any employee of the railroad to lend me any assistance in reason for which I might ask.

As the grade of the track was quite high and steep it was late afternoon, even by the help of a half dozen husky section men, before we had the car up on the ties. I was then told that a train was due within less than an hour, and that we had better make haste across the thousand-feet-long trestle bridge spanning the roaring current which raced some thirty or more feet below. As I expected to cross in fifteen or twenty minutes, I sent my wife across on the hand car with the section foreman and his gang, which was composed of reliable-looking Swedes.

A storm had been threatening for a couple of hours and by the time we were less than half way across the bridge, bumping very carefully and very slowly across, with less than eight inches between the tires on one side and the abyss below, the storm broke with intense fury. The first blasts were so strong that I feared at first that we would be blown off the trestle, there being no guard rail or other protection. In a few minutes the rain began falling in sheets and the lightning played in continuous flashes. The wet rubber tires and the wet ties made a combination which, in connection with the horizontal sheets of pelting rain, made our situation worse than precarious, especially when we could not forget that a train was soon due in a direction opposite to that we were going.

My driver got so nervous that I took the wheel and he walked ahead a tie at the time, turning and motioning to right or left by signaling with his hands in order to keep me going straight ahead and not to slip overside. This, of course, was mighty slow work and the tension became almost strong enough to have unstrung anybody's nerves. It seemed to me that we had been hours jolting along since we entered the trestle, when I distinctly heard the whistle of a train in a lull of the storm, though either on account of the storm or a curve I could not see the headlights. Screaming to the driver to run ahead as fast as he could and never mind me, I stepped on the accelerator with a silent prayer on my lips, and the car shot ahead the short remaining distance of the trestle, and then we could see the headlights of the approaching locomotive. With the aid of a small board the car cleared the track and landed in the ditch just as the train shot by with a scream and a roar which sounded positively unearthly, combined as it was with the noise of the storm. My wife, who was numb with fright, maintained afterwards that the hoarse roar and clatter of the speeding locomotive sounded to her as a scream of baffled rage and disappointment uttered by some giant supernatural evil monster.

While this experience was almost melodramatic, it ended with a touch of humor which soon made us forget our dangerous adventure. The section hands willingly lent us their aid, though drenched to the skin as we all were, and in a short time we were ready to proceed. I knew that the trail should be a short distance—say a quarter of a mile or less—to the left, so headed cross country in that direction. Probably on account of the blinding rain I missed the trail and finally we decided to stop, eat some crackers and sardines from our commissary, and snatch what sleep we could in our wet clothes while remaining in the seats of the car, as erecting camp in such weather was impracticable.

When daylight broke we found on looking through the curtains, that we were less than a hundred feet from the door of a ranch house, the only house from miles around. Kind providence had guided us to a safe and comfortable haven, as the folks of the ranch most hospitably took us in and afforded us an opportunity to dry our clothes and regaled us with a wonderful breakfast of flapjacks, eggs and coffee. We spent the balance of the day and the next night here, in order to give the soil a chance to dry before again proceeding, and besides we needed the rest after our nerve-racking experience.

A fine highway bridge now spans the Powder River where the ford was, as similar bridges now afford safe crossings over the larger rivers on practically all the main transcontinental motor routes.

Indian Slough

On taking the first truck on a transcontinental hike we had eventually, after all sorts of hardships and experiences which at times seemed almost to block our efforts to succeed in our undertaking, reached the banks of the Colorado River at Ehrenburg, California, the goal and reward for all our strenuous adventures on the trip, was only just across a comparatively narrow stream, and yet so far away that we for a while despaired of reaching it. As at that time there were no highway bridges across the Colorado either at Needles or Yuma, I had laid our course for Ehrenburg in order to cross by the ferry at that point, believing from a previous experience with it that it would be large enough to get our seven-ton truck across.

However, we learned upon reaching the little river town, after crossing the desert from Phoenix, that the large flat-bottomed scow, which in connection with a gasoline launch had constituted the ferry when I crossed here a few months previously, had been swept away by a flood and that only a very much smaller scow or float was available. The citizens of the little burg, which consisted of three saloons and a store, maintained that there would be no use attempting to take the truck across with the available equipment, but on looking the outfit over carefully I decided to risk it.

The first two trips across took our load of gasoline and oil barrels, lumber and much paraphernalia with which we were provided in order to overcome difficulties; also seats, hood and all parts of the engine which could be removed, in order to lighten the final load. With great care the truck itself was finally gotten aboard, and almost swamped the little scow with its weight. The current was so swift that we had to proceed up stream close to the Arizona bank for more than a mile before we dared to attempt shooting across. We were a mighty anxious crew when the ferryman headed his launch towards the center of the stream and his Indian helpers with long sweeps steered a course diagonally across.

Luck was with us and we made the promised land in safety, but found great difficulty in discovering a favorable landing place on the brush-grown bank of the river. However, at least we were ashore, in the thick brush, it is true, but the solid earth underneath our feet felt good. While the Indians chopped away the brush to enable us to get away us to get away from the bank of the stream the rest of us got busy assembling our outfit, which took us twenty-four hours to accomplish. Less than half a mile from the river we met our greatest disappointment, which looked to us like a real Waterloo. A recent overflow of the river had left enough water in a large depression or slough to form a veritable lake, dotted with huge trees and about five feet deep in the center. It extended for miles up and down parallel to the river and, as the bottom was a slimy ooze, there really seemed nothing to do at first but to sit down for a few weeks and let the slough dry up by the slow method of evaporation.

After studying the situation for a while, I partly disrobed, made a bundle of my clothes, and with this on my head waded and swam across the ill-smelling water, which was almost thick with decayed vegetable matter. Calling to my companions that I would be gone two or three hours and for them to amuse themselves as best they could by playing tag with the millions of mosquitoes which drifted about in clouds. I dressed and proceeded to the town of Blythe, a private irrigation project, four miles distant. It being Sunday, I found a dozen men about with nothing to do but take it easy after the week's work. As they constituted the chamber of commerce of the embryonic metropolis, I laid our predicament before them and received the proffer of all the mules and steel cable, formerly used for well-drilling, that I might stand in need of if I could show them how to succeed in getting the heavy truck across the mucky bottom of the slough.

To tell the truth, I did not have much faith in accomplishing the task, but, making up my mind that the truck might as well perish by drowning as we from mosquito bites, I assumed an air of confidence and we brought the mules and paraphernalia to the edge of the slough, which was some six hundred feet wide at the narrowest point. I realized that it would be useless to try to haul the heavy vehicle across the soft bottom by a direct pull and that multiplying block and tackle had to be rigged. This was difficult to accomplish on account of the big trees in the slough, which necessitated a zigzag course.

We buried a dead-man in the trail. For the benefit of those that do not know the meaning of this rather gruesome phraseology, I will explain that a dead-man means a stout leg buried at some depth across the direction of the pull. To this the long steel cable was fastened, to serve as an anchor against which to exert the force of the pull. Then another swim across the nasty pool to superintend the fastening of the block and tackle to the front axle and to the first tree, which stood in the water about a hundred feet from the edge and directly in the path chosen for our crossing. When all was ready four mules were hitched to the cable, and the word was passed to go ahead. Slowly the big truck, from which of course had been removed magneto and carburetor, moved ahead and gradually dipped deeper and deeper into the slimy water.

When it was nearing the tree to which the tackle was fastened, the mules had walked over four hundred feet from the dead man and we had to make a new hitch, lengthening the tackle-ropes and making fast to another tree, at a different angle and another hundred feet ahead. To make this new hitch was no easy undertaking, as it had to be done an arm-length underwater; but soon we again proceeded. Deeper and deeper the truck went down, until by the time another new hitch had become necessary the top of the radiator and hood was just awash. To make the change of hitch on the front axle this time was quite another proposition, as two men had to entirely submerge themselves to accomplish it. It took a long time, but it was finally done and again we moved ahead, still going deeper for every foot.

When for the third time the tackle-ropes had to be lengthened, the water reached the knees of the man who sat in the driver's high seat to steer. After five different changes in our course and procuring new hitches, we eventually pulled up on the coveted shore. The big vehicle was received by a hearty cheer from all throats and we all felt that we had accomplished a real feat. The men from Blythe went home and in three hours we followed under our own power, little the worse for our experience except that the truck was covered by ill-smelling filth and we all stood much in need of a bath, which we duly took by the bucketful at the town pump.

I learned that the swamp was called the Indian Slough, and I do not think that anyone connected with taking the truck across it will ever forget the experience.

The Gospel and Good Roads

In many sections of the West the most energetic workers for the Good Roads movement are the clergy. The gospel of good roads is consistently being preached by these ministers, be they Protestant or Catholic, and as these workers wield a potent influence in their respective sections, they prove an especially valuable aid in intelligently convincing their fellow citizens of the value and local economics of improved highways. And let me say right here I have found these men the best of scouts and congenial companions on many a strenuous pathfinding trip.

The Rev. Father Vabre, at Flagstaff, Arizona, he of the sunny smile and ever-unruffled disposition, has scouted all over and Northern Arizona with me among whites and Indians. He has been a powerful factor in helping to bring about the result that today the National Old Trails route is graded and provided with substantial concrete bridges across canyons and sandy washes through a considerable part of his sphere of influence. And it must be remembered that this is a sparsely settled region, there often being forty miles between settlements and no houses between. The Rev. Father De Richemont, at St. John's, in central Eastern Arizona, a scholarly man of great influence in his section, has also been a powerful help towards the improvement of the road in his vicinity.

In New Mexico the Rev. Dr. H. M. Shields, of Dawson, has taken an unusually active part in bringing about road betterment in a region where the people were peculiarly influenced by the leadership of their spiritual adviser. The Rev. Dr. S. M. Johnson, of Roswell, New Mexico, has become an interstate preacher of the good-roads gospel. He is ever willing to travel any distance to attend meetings where boosters are organizing bodies for the improvement of highways. As he is a scholarly, eloquent man, with a thorough knowledge of his subject, results of a satisfactory nature usually follow in his wake.

Over in Texas, the Rev. Dr. T. P. Grant, of Brady, has stumped the whole State in advocacy of road-bond issues, and to what end may be judged by the fact that Texas has invested millions in road improvements and the good work is still going on. Dr. Grant was one of the best companions on a motor hike I have ever had the pleasure to meet.

Over in Colorado, there is a quiet, reserved Catholic priest at Idaho Springs, the Rev. Father McCabe, than whom none has worked harder, and with more splendid results to develop the Berthoud Pass route of the Midland Trail, the Roosevelt National Highway. The elimination of the steep and rough grade across Floyd Hill on this route and the building of a good State highway through this section must be placed to the credit of Father McCabe.

I could keep on mentioning specific instances in nearly all of the Western States of the well-directed zeal of clergymen towards similar satisfactory local results. It is merely my intention in this chapter to acknowledge the splendid cooperation of these men and to call well-merited attention to and show appreciation of their unselfish public spiritedness.

Kicking Up the Dust of Ages

Our wonderful Southwest is unquestionably one of the most interesting regions of the United States, looked at from any number of angles. Certainly I have found it of absorbing interest in my pathfinding trips. As its twenty-six Indian pueblos, every one a self-governing little republic, inhabited by self-supporting and self-respecting folks, living the life of their ancestors for uncounted generations, as well as its nearly a dozen Indian tribes living on reservations, its turbulent history, its ancient civilization, its scenery, climate and resources, are recounted in my book, "Through the Land of Yesterday," I will here only briefly mention some of the prehistoric ruins in that region.

At various places adjacent to the National Old Trails route in New Mexico and Arizona, and reached by ancient trails, some of them too rough for motor cars, are many of the most interesting archaeological remains in the world. The wonder of it is that these are comparatively little known—in fact, practically unknown—to the vastly greater proportion of Americans. And yet quite a number of them are easily reached by motor car and are close to settled communities.

Thus the wonderful ruins of the vast communal house of Tyu'onyi are located in the canyon of Rito de los Frijoles, only thirty-five miles from Santa Fe, itself probably the most picturesquely interesting city in the United States and the second oldest. This communal house contained originally seven hundred rooms and was a true prototype of the modern city apartment house. Nearby in the same canyon are hundreds of cliff and cave dwellings which tell the student of archaeology about a civilization reaching so far back into the hoary prehistoric past that even no conjectures as to their age are ventured by the learned men who dig, excavate, study and draw conclusions from the pottery, skeletons, basketry and other remains of those who once upon a time occupied these tiny dwellings. The kiva, or sacred ceremonial underground chamber, excavated on a shelf a hundred and fifty feet up the sheer cliff side of the canyon, is a rare treat to visit. This region forms the Bandolier National Monument, and the Government custodian, Judge Abbott, will most cheerfully guide anyone up to this venerable eyrie.

It is said that about twenty thousand prehistoric ruins and cave-dwellings are located in the Santa Fe region, some of the most interesting of which, in addition to those in Rito de lose Frijoles are Puye, Tsankawi, Navawi and Tcherge.

At Chaco Canyon, northeast of Gallup, there are some ten great ruins the largest of which is Pueblo Bonito, with more than a thousand rooms.

On the Navaho Indian reservation in Arizona there are a number of most wonderful ruins, as those of the justly famous scenic Canyon de Chelly, near Chinle, forty miles north of Fort Defiance. Here are about two hundred ruins, of which the "White House," conspicuously white against the somber background of a shallow cave, is best known. Also within less than thirty miles from the trading post of Tyende or Kayenta are three remarkable ruins: Betatakin, a veritable city in a splendid state of preservation, and only discovered about ten years ago; Inscription House, an ancient ruin, in one room of which is found an inscription scratched on the wall by some prowling, adventurous member of one of the roving bands of Spaniards who in the sixteenth century ventured far into the most remote corners of the Spanish province of New Grenada, as the country was then called, in search of fabled treasure: Keet-seel, or pottery house, a ruin clinging to the very side of a precipitous cliff. These three ruins constitute the Navaho National Monument.

In the southwest portion of Colorado are the Hovenweap ruins, not yet excavated but said to be especially interesting. Not far away is the Mesa Verde National Park, jutting into the Southern Ute Indian reservation. This region is reached via the Spanish Trail-Mesa Verde Highway from Pueblo and contains some of the most wonderful ruins of the entire Southwest. The most conspicuous among these are the Cliff Palace, Spruce Tree House, Balcony House, Sun Temple and Peabody House, all excavated and accessible. Near the town of Aztec, in northeastern New Mexico, on the same highway and not far from Mesa Verde, are the Aztec ruins now in course of exploration and said to be of paramount interest.

One of the most beautifully situated prehistoric ruins in Arizona is that of the Tonto National Monument, a mile south of the Apache Trail and only five miles east of Roosevelt Dam. These ruins are especially easy of access and are located up the side of a canyon which in itself is a veritable garden of numerous varieties of beautiful desert cactus. The light color of these ruins contrast so conspicuously with the dark cave back of them that, from a distance, they have the appearance of bright marble structures. Montezuma Castle, south of Flagstaff, is another ruin of splendid picturesqueness. Then there are the easily accessible cliff dwellings in Walnut Canyon, only nine miles from Flagstaff, many ruins of large community houses near Tempe and Mesa, in the Salt River valley, and literally thousands of smaller ruins scattered throughout the entire northern part of New Mexico and Arizona.

Indeed, searching for possible automobile routes in this entrancing "Land of Yesterday" was literally kicking up the dust of ages along prehistoric trails, often alongside paths worn ankle deep by the moccasined feet of countless generations of forgotten races. And to think some of our people go to Egypt and other eastern countries, drawn there by the magnet of the mystery of the ancient, when we have in our own country ruins rivaling in interest and probably in age those of any country on the Mediterranean. If they want the foreign flavor, surely the language, costumes and customs of the swarthy races of our own scenic archaeological and ethnological attractions which they deserve and which will someday be done. Then the harvest of gold from the restless roaming tourist will surpass the combined returns from all the other resources of the Southwest.

Sectional Rivalry

In unity there is strength. This old adage is often lost sight of by rival contenders from the honor of being located on a particular trunk-line motor route which may be projected through a section of country where either one of two or more communities may offer equal advantages for the location of such a route. While a healthy and sportsmanlike rivalry is commendable and frequently causes the building of two routes where only one was in contemplation, it is unfortunately too often the case that this rivalry assumes the nature of acrimonious recriminations and causes such a hatred and intolerable situation that a route has been located through a territory where its location would benefit neither contestant. An award of this kind, with which I have been identified more than once, reminds one of the situation some years ago in Arizona, when Prescott and Tucson fought so hard and with such bitterness for the location of the State capital that Phoenix was chosen as a compromise, thus causing both the contenders to lose out.

Well-known examples of sectional rivalry between cities are those of Seattle and Portland, Minneapolis and St. Paul, Dallas and Fort Worth, and San Francisco and Los Angeles. In the latter case the feeling has spread so that now it is Northern California against Southern California, to the serious detriment of the whole State. It is often claimed that the Californians are a mighty self-opinionated lot and rather hold that they are the tail that wags the dog, meaning the rest of the United States, and that this sectional pride is about the only thing upon which the Northern and Southern Californians agree.

Personally, I think that California as a unit and an integral part of these great United States would find it altogether to its advantage to pull together in all things, as the State has riches and glories enough to go around and to spare. It can well afford to reach out the welcome hand of hospitality to all visitors, whatever part of the State they enter first, and its citizens, as Californians, not Southern or Northern Californians, place every facility at their disposal to visit the many wonderful attractions all over the State. I think that the development of a network of good highways within the commonwealth, a matter upon which the two sections seem to agree and cooperate, will eventually do away with any sectional bitterness and will bring about a tolerance and unity of general efforts which must inevitably rebound to the great benefit of all sections.

Texas is so cumbersomely unwieldy that it is not closely enough knitted together on many matters that should be made the concern of all parts of the State. This is largely due to the climatic differences and consequent conflicting interests of its extreme sections, where the climate ranges from the sub-tropical of the gulf coast to the severe winters of the plains. Again the improvement of highways, which will make intercommunication between the most remote corners of the vast commonwealth easy and cause a better understanding of the problems in each section, will eventually make one entity of them all and cause them to present a solid front, one for all and all for one, when problems of Statewide importance arise.

Colorado is divided into two parts, the plains and the "Western Slope," the Rocky Mountains being the natural barrier between the two. In addition, an acrimonious jealousy has in the past existed between Denver, Colorado Springs and Pueblo, all of them located on the east slope, where the plains and mountains meet. It has been claimed that the altitude at which these cities lie causes people to become high-strung or irritable and thus quarrelsome, and, as everyone knows, there is no quarrel more bitter than a family quarrel. However, I am happy to be able to record that since the advent of the good-roads era, when nearly all parts of the State on both sides of the mountains are easily accessible by motor car, this sectional rivalry and jealousy has almost entirely disappeared. It has been found that there is enough tourist traffic to satisfy every town, and more coming every year; hence Coloradans are now all putting their shoulders to the same wheel and heave together for the glory of and to the great benefit of the State. The splendid roads through their magnificent mountain region enable tourists to roam at will and enjoy a climate and scenery which are sure to induce them to stay longer than at first intended and to come again. All Colorado needs to do is to treat its visitors fairly, without greed, and its attractions will prove more valuable than all its mineral wealth.

In the Northwest, the States of Wyoming, Montana, Idaho and Washington pull together like a trained team of horses, and this unity of effort is increasingly effective in bringing to the attention of money-spending travelers the many delights of this region. These efforts are, of course, much strengthened by the location of the Yellowstone, Glacier and Mt. Rainier national parks within this region. The glad hand of welcome, hospitality and fair treatment are bringing about results in the Northwest which the gradual expansion of good-roads systems is sure to increase to such a volume of tourist's traffic that all communities will be benefited. Many sections of the United States could learn much to their advantage by studying and following the example of the nonwestern States.

Now we come to Arizona and New Mexico. No one can accuse these States of being unprogressive or inhospitable, in fact, their characteristics are all to the contrary. Nevertheless it is undeniable that most communities in these commonwealths must be called to a large degree somewhat indifferent or at least lethargic in the matter of exerting special efforts to make the unquestionably most wonderful attractions of these States known to the outside world. They are generally perfectly willing that outsiders do this work for them or indifferent as to how it is done so it does not cost themselves special efforts or money. In saying this I know whereof I speak. It is doubtful if Arizona and New Mexico has had a better friend than myself. I have for years traveled through their territory, have written widely of the wonderful attractions, scenically, archeologically and otherwise, of these States in magazines and books. While I have always met with a welcome, I have, on the other hand, received little or no cooperation in the exploitations of their attractions nor in fact noted any special appreciation of my efforts in their behalf except from the little town of Springerville, Arizona. The noted writer, Charles F. Lummis, calls this country "the land of tomorrow," and perhaps these folks of the southwest will cooperate "tomorrow." Quien sabe?

On the other hand it is a hopeful omen that Arizona and New Mexico have made a good start in the building of roads that are fast making its attractions, some of which are unmatched anywhere on earth, easily accessible to motor tourists. The wonderful pueblos of the Rio Grande valley, the interesting prehistoric ruins of community houses and cliff dwellings, the many Indian tribes with their ceremonial dances, the Painted Desert, petrified forests, natural monuments, the Grand Canyon, the National Forests, the magnetic attractions of the Gila Desert, the Roosevelt and Elephant Butte irrigation dams, the fine fishing streams and hunting grounds and numerous other features to be found in these States, are nowadays within the reach of any red-blooded motor tourists. To increase the volume of the lucrative tourist traffic it is only necessary to make some intelligent and united effort to call the attention of the world to these attractions, and if this is done on a liberal scale these States will find their publicity efforts rewarded by an unprecedented stream of wealth rolling in on them.

In this country the example of the New England States may be studied to good effect by Arizona and New Mexico, and if they should care to go further afield for more intensive studies, Italy, France and Switzerland would present many a wholesome lesson.

Westgard photographed this American Automobile Association representative on a transcontinental trip passing a rare road sign near Glendive, MT, in 1912. (National Archives)

Out West

One of the most remarkable observations that one is forced to make when traveling around in the eastern part of our country is the limited comprehension of the vast size and resources of the United States, often displayed by people whom one really expects to have a wider knowledge of the subject. I do not refer to the army of Americans of wealth, who can glibly tell you all about even the more remote corners of Europe, but who have never seen California, the Grand Canyon or the wonders of our National Parks, and either look rather bored at being told about them or look as if a recital of their beauties and wonders must be patiently endured or merely considered one of the expected "boasts" of their countrymen. One of the good things following the world war was the fact that as Europe was closed to these folks they were literally compelled, being people of leisure with few serious objects in life aside from traveling, to visit regions in the United States which they heretofore had thought too arduous to approach.

This circumstance has brought an appreciation of their own wonderful country that has made them at the same time prouder Americans and staunch advocates of the "See America first" gospel. It is, however, the solid "middle class" people (as they are sometimes called), the farmer and tradesman, that frequently show such gross ignorance of the United States that one wonders at it in these days of compulsory schooling. It would be ridiculous if it were not such an evidence of smug indifference. Of course these conditions will mend in proportion as these people acquire the ownership of a motor car. This blessing of modern times, in my opinion, is proving itself the greatest educator in history, because its use compels acquiring knowledge, first of one's own section, then of one's own State and finally, as the network of good roads spreads, of one's entire country, besides broadening one's vision of life and appreciation of the problems facing other regions outside of one's own. This education will have a powerful influence on our politics and tend to cultivate toleration and sympathy, and at the same time it will wipe out sectionalism.

I well remember when once in the early days of motordom, the time when roads were all dirt roads and one spent more than half of his time on his back underneath the car, and thirty miles was considered quite a day's ride, I stopped at a farmhouse in eastern Connecticut to borrow some tools from a farmer, which I needed in tinkering with the car, the conversation turned on "Out West." I mentioned having traveled through our western states, but, of course, not in those early days, by motor. The farmer, rather conscious of some traveling himself, remarked that he also had been "Out West," to visit a brother that a generation before had moved there. More for the purpose of seeming polite than for any real interest in the subject, I asked him what part of the west he had visited. To my utter amazement he proudly said, "in York State, near Utica."

As a matter of fact this man was quite a traveler when one compared him with the thousands upon thousands of sturdy Americans who, at least up to very recent times, had never been outside of their own county, to say nothing of their State. Ingrown sectionalism and indifference to the welfare or needs of fellow citizens beyond their own narrow sphere of vision is traceable directly to this condition. Of all the modern methods of communication, telegraphy, telephone, rural delivery or mail, interurban electric cars, railroad, newspapers and magazines, the strongest and most potent antidote to ignorance is the motor car, because it teaches while it gives pleasure and health, and thus is "easy to take."

Convict Labor

Our immensely fast-growing demand for improved highways which call for the expenditure of hundreds of millions of dollars annually, has caused such a scarcity of labor, or the class which can be utilized for this purpose, that many of the States in the Union are using convicts to help fill the pressing want. In spite of the fact that no State has enough inmates in its penal institutions, who can properly be used for roadwork, to affect the labor market, labor organizations have in some States selfishly adopted the rule of the dog in the manger and through politics prevented the utilization of convict labor on highway work or other public improvements. This stand not only does not benefit these organizations, but retards the construction of highways important to the State and deprives fellow human beings, often doing penance for relatively slight offences against society, or the outdoor life and healthy exercise that help to purify mind and body and fit them for better life when their terms are expired.

There are two methods employed in applying convict labor to roadwork, the honor system, best exemplified in Colorado, where it was first introduced, and the system where the convicts work in striped suits, often weighted down by chains and guarded by men with cocked rifles, and herded into wheeled cages at night like wild beasts.

Let us first consider how the honor system, so idealistically conceived with humanitarian purposes in view, really works in practice. Warden Tynan, of the Colorado State penitentiary at Canon City, must be given the credit of first using the honor system. Much needed improvements of highways across the mountain passes were so delayed and hampered by lack of labor that the State resolved to try the application of Mr. Tynan's scheme. Briefly this consisted in allowing short term prisoners and trustees the privilege of living in healthy camps, working in the bracing pure air, using ordinary civilian clothes in place of the degrading prison uniforms, laboring without armed guards, and in addition being allowed a small daily wage for their work, thus laying up something against the day of release. From the standpoint of the State this accomplished much to be desired: the carrying on of needed improvements, making the convict earn his keep in place of being an expense to the commonwealth, and improving his morale so that when released he will be a better citizen and not as liable to again offend against the statute laws. From the standpoint of the convict the outdoor life, the escape from the confining prison walls, the healthy exercise, good food and the confidence shown in him by this unguarded and un-uniformed life make him see life in brighter colors and create better intentions for the future. As a result there has been practically no efforts to escape, and in the one or two cases which have occurred, the culprits who broke their given words in this respect have, when caught, been ostracized by their fellow prisoners and deprived of the privilege of further outdoor work. This punishment has proved more potent than solitary confinement and other harsh means of handling recalcitrant offenders against prison rules. I have on occasions visited Colorado convict road camps and joined the men at their meals. Their freedom from restraint or mental depression was most noticeable. They acted and talked naturally like free men. The benefits of this system was so evident that it needed no obtuse or statistical arguments to convince anyone.

Now let us look at the other method of using convict labor as practiced in some of the older southern states. This picture here is of a very different character. On one of my trips of investigation of routes to Florida some years ago, I encountered several convict road camps in three different states. At one of these camps a white man, the only one in the camp aside from the guards, was working among a gang of burly negroes. Upon inquiry I learned that his offense had been the terrible crime of getting drunk. And for this he, a Southerner with a Southerner's prejudice of acknowledging equality or associating with negroes, was made to suffer the, to him, unspeakable indignity of working in a chain gang of black men. After talking with him for some moments, I was convinced that this galling treatment had caused such a resentment in his otherwise normal mind that he stood in danger of becoming a confirmed criminal and foe of society when he again had his freedom.

Among the dozen negro convicts at work at this camp five were serving life sentences, and consequently had no fear of taking chances of getting away, as they would be no worse off if they failed of success in the attempt. This gang was served with water by a diminutive negro boy, apparently some ten or eleven years old and, it seems almost unbelievable, this little chap had not only iron chains running from a metal belt around his waist to iron rings about both his ankles, but carried a heavy iron ball, which was chained to his wrist on one hand, while with the other he carried the waterbucket. I learned upon inquiry that he was so treated because he was a confirmed thief, or at least, as one guard put it, "liable to pilfer anything." Many of the prisoners had the waist-to-ankle chains, and all were dressed in conspicuous black and white striped suits and caps. Guards with shouldered rifles patrolled the roadside. At night these unfortunate beings, having served as a show for all passers along the road during the day, were confined in stout iron-barred cages on wheels which were moved along as the work progressed.

The contrast between the two methods of utilizing convict labor here described is overwhelming. Both in applications and effect they differ as light from darkness, as virtue from depravity.

Westgard photographed a team of horses pulling a stuck car through a sandy wash onto a mesa near Yuma, CA, in 1913. Convict labor was not used. (National Archives)

At the Grand Canyon

Six years ago I visited the Grand Canyon of Arizona for the first time in a motor car. At that time only an occasional local car from Flagstaff and one or two long-distance cars had ever been there. There were no garage accommodations and no gasoline or oil to be had there at that time. As I did not care to leave my car outdoors over night on account of various valuable instruments of a scientific character, I persuaded the manager of El Tovar Hotel to arrange for its accommodation in the carriage barn.

When I urged the manager to take steps to provide an up-to-date garage as motorists were sure to come in ever increasing numbers in my footsteps, or rather tire-tracks, he maintained that the management did not care for that kind of patronage, and anyway there would not be many motorists braving the wilds of Arizona.

Two years later I again came to the Grand Canyon by motor car, and what did I find? A large garage with modern equipment, which had that summer housed over twelve hundred cars. Furthermore, a large extension was being constructed to take care of the increasing tourist traffic arriving by motor car. And the management was mighty glad to see them coming too.

Since the Grand Canyon has been made a National Park and will be connected with the National Old Trails Road with a good highway swarms of motor tourists will in coming years annually visit this most impressive natural scenery on the face of the globe, especially after some way has been found to pump water from the Colorado River in the bottom of the chasm to the rim, so that motor car campers may be properly cared for.

Hazing the Lord

On one of my many trips across the United States we were accompanied by an Englishman who was much interested in gathering "impressions" of the United States. He was a quiet, somewhat reserved young gentleman of very precise manners and was by us promptly called the Lord, for short. Out in Kansas some of the local people played a few innocent jokes on him, which he took in the best manner possible. Among these were such instances as inducing him to give a fourth of July speech to a large audience in a public park of one of the towns and allowing him the valued privilege of jerking open the door of the den whence the "usual" badger was supposed to rush out and engage in mortal combat with a "fierce" mongrel, a rather hackneyed practical joke practiced on tyro tenderfeet.

Down in Arizona he ventured the remark in a conversation with some local people that he had surely expected the West to be more "woolly," and that so far he had not seen a single one of the desperadoes, road-agents, gamblers and cut-throats which he had read about, and which were expected to roam about freely and ply their trade with impunity. The good people of Arizona were not going to let such a blot on their reputation remain, and staged a regular wild-west holdup, which was successfully pulled off in the southeast part of the state. In the most approved fashion two masked horsemen rode out from behind large boulders alongside the trail in a desolate section, and with leveled "six-guns" demanded "your money or your life." Of course everybody was in the joke but the Lord, so everybody elevated their hands, and like good sports, stood for having their loose change abstracted from their pockets.

When the car arrived at the next town it was met by a committee, among whom were the two "robbers." At the hotel bar the Englishman's money, a modest sum, was freely spent on the visitors and everybody was happy, none more so than our foreign guest who told most circumstantially of the adventure, and cabled an account of it to London. He never did learn the real facts of the case, and even today is of the opinion that after all the west is some country for red-blooded experiences.

Colorado Mutton

Arriving at a Colorado ranch on one of my trips, the owner apologized for having nothing in the house but mutton to serve us. We assured him that mutton was certainly all right, and that we had brought our appetites with us. When the meal was served I discovered that the "mutton" was venison, and as I realized that it was the closed season for shooting deer, I praised the mutton and simulated ignorance of the real character of the food which, of course, was just what we were all expected to do. Not so our driver, who kept insisting that he had never tasted such mutton, and that it was the best he had ever eaten, but wanted to know what breed of sheep produced such juicy, palatable meat. Seeing that he would not be satisfied till he had the information safely tucked away in his head, the rancher told him, without a smile, that it was Rocky Mountain sheep. The driver often spoke of the delicious mutton produced in Colorado from the mountain sheep.

The Queen of the Desert

At one of the small towns on the National Old Trails road in the Mohave Desert, there lived a curious character, an old woman, generally called "Mama, queen of the desert." She was one of the pioneer "desert rats," who came in with a prospecting party and settled in a small shanty town near the railroad. She opened a small store and looked after the occasional traveler who ventured into or came back from the Death Valley region, a mythical Eldorado, where gold was supposed to be plenty as berries on an elderberry bush, but whence most of hardy prospectors, who hazarded the dangers of the trail into it, came back empty handed and often half demented with the sufferings endured in this well-named region. Many did not come back at all, and their bleached bones are whitening the floor of this terrible country, more than two hundred feet below sea level. To those who came back "Mama" was the good Samaritan, and in spite of her uncouth ways and careless garb was to them a glorified being.

One night we arrived at this little settlement about ten o'clock, hungry and weary after a hot day's ride through the desert. As we wiggled out way through the deep sand of the main (and only) street, there appeared in the full glare of our headlights a woman, barefooted and calico-mother-hubbard- dressed, who stopped in the middle of the track and kept waving her arms excitedly. This proved to the "queen of the desert," of whom I had heard. She informed us that we had better stop over for the night, and that she could furnish us with good beds. She evidently was not going to let anyone get by without at least being apprised of the accommodations available.

Assuring her that her hospitality was appreciated and would be accepted, I inquired about something to eat. To our disappointment she said there was no chance of appeasing our hunger until next day, when what she called "the hash-house," otherwise the restaurant, opened. I maintained that would not do at all, and "guessed" I could find something to eat somewhere, aside from the crackers and cheese which she finally offered us from the stock in the store. Evidently feeling that she knew her ground, she offered to bet that I could not, the stake being free beds or beds at double rate, according to who should win.

Without taking up this sporting proposition, I approached a house, from the window of which shone the only light apparent in the town. This proved to be the railroad station with a telegraph operator on duty. Explaining to him our predicament he handed me a key and told me it would unlock the third house down the street. Here we would find an oil-burner cook stove and food in the pantry, ham, eggs, rolls, jam, and other good things. We were welcome to help ourselves and he only regretted he could not leave his post to come over and cook it for us in his bachelor home.

"Mama" seemed much surprised at the result of my foraging expedition. While she went to prepare the beds we cooked a very satisfying meal in the home of this true gentleman of the wide places, who had shown such hospitality to strangers. He absolutely refused any recompense for the food consumed. We could only pay him with our thanks. Next morning "Mama" like a true sport, refused pay for her beds, because she had lost the wager, even though it had not been accepted by me. No argument could induce her to change her decision in this respect.

Queen Victoria

While passing through Georgia on the Dixie Highway, we put up at the only hotel in one of the smaller towns. My wife inquired of the clerk if there was a chance to have some laundry done the next day, which we had planned to spend at this town. She was assured that it would be promptly arranged. Early next morning the clerk sent word up that Queen Victoria was down stairs and he should send her up. Having for the moment forgotten about the laundry, and thinking that this was supposed to be a joke at my instigation, my wife said she would be much honored to have her majesty grace our humble quarters with her presence.

In a few minutes a knock sounded on the door and my wife swung it wide open. There stood a coal-black negro woman with a wide grin showing gleaming white teeth and white of her eyes shining like two stars. Clutching her dress, one on each side were two tiny pickaninnies some four or five years old, curiosity and wonder depicted on their curly-topped little black faces. The woman said she was Queen Victoria, the laundress. The two kids were twins and named Abraham Lincoln and Jefferson Davis, while upon inquiry it was learned that the husband's name was George Washington. These were all given names, the family name being Munroe. Truly a historic and distinguished family, I should say.

Tickling the Carburetor

In making our way up a water-bar-infested steep road in the Green mountains of Vermont, we overtook a small car which was bucking its way in spasms, leaps and bounds ahead of us. At a place where the road curved, I noticed an old gentleman at the steering wheel, while a woman was breathlessly running beside the car, the hood of which was thrown back on one side. She had her arm stretched in under the hood and had quite a task keeping up with the erratic pace of the "horseless carriage," anxiety being plainly depicted on her face, which was grimy from perspiration and lubricating grease. Having attained the top of the grade she sat down at the roadside to rest, and I asked her why on earth she was doing the marathon and acrobatics on such a hot day and on such steep ground. With the most amusing expression of annoyance on her face she said that she did not see that the reason was any of my business, but it I wanted particularly to know, it was no family secret, and she was only "tickling" the carburetor.

Later I saw the same pair leaving from the front of a barn which served as a garage in a small town, the old gentleman with a grim and determined expression of do or die on his face and his hands grasping the steering wheel like grim death till his knuckles showed white, while the little woman was cranking away for dear life, till she finally succeeded in starting "the pesky thing."

'Ware Handshaking

The Pueblo Indian either in order to show his friendliness or to indicate his familiarity with the white man's ways, I am not sure which, always insists on shaking hands when first meeting a white person, though I have never noticed him practice this custom among his own people. Unfortunately, a great many individuals of various tribes inhabiting the twenty-six scattered Pueblos of the Southwest are inflicted with trachoma, a contagious and reputedly incurable eye disease. For this reason all visitors to one of these little self-governing republics should use extreme care not to indulge in handshaking with the inhabitants promiscuously.

On one occasion when we visited one of the Pueblos near Santa Fe, the cacique after vigorously shaking my gloved hand, went up to the car and stretched out his hand to my wife, who had not yet had time to put on her gloves when she saw him coming. Catching my eye she tucked her hands under the lap robe and made the excuse that she had a bruised finger, a necessary subterfuge in this case, as the man was nearly blind with trachoma. Most of his family were similarly afflicted, and they all wanted to shake hands. We had to use great care in our trips, which extended to all the Indian tribes in New Mexico and Arizona, and almost everywhere we found the red-lidded filmy eyes which indicate the presence of this dangerous disease. However, by taking proper precautions in the way of gloved hands and the use of disinfectants, the danger of infection may be avoided.

Prospectors

One of the most interesting characters one meets in the arid regions of the southwest is the prospector. He is nearly always the personification of sunny optimism, especially the confirmed specimen of the species. I have spent many a pleasant evening at the campfire listening to the tales of fortune "almost found" by some of the old dyed-in-the-wool roamers of the desert.

At one time we pitched camp at Winter's well on the Harquahala Plain between Phoenix and the Colorado river, and as were busy about getting our supper ready, there came into the light of the campfire a diminutive burro laden down with grub sacks, picks and shovels. Immediately following was an old man of three score and ten years or more, who asked to share our fire with us, as the custom is in remote regions. Being assured that he was welcome, he busied himself preparing his frugal meal and was delighted when we offered him some fruits and spuds, as potatoes are generally called in that country. After our repast and with the pipes drawing well, the atmosphere very naturally called for tales of his wanderings, and he proved a very interesting raconteur. For more than forty-five years he had roamed the mountain and desert regions between Canada and Mexico, and claimed to have located several fine mines, but always somebody else got away with the big fortunes made by these strikes, while he only received a few hundred dollars. However, he had a strong hunch that there was gold at a certain place not far distant and was sure that he would be able to uncover it, and this time he would take care that no one cheated him out of it. Would I be interested in backing him in his search, it would only take a modest sum, a few hundred dollars? Having received many similar invitations on other occasions to grub-stake some of these consistent dreamers, who had sure things and would inevitably located them "tomorrow," I found an excuse to decline the flattering offer. He did not seem the least disappointed at this, but regaled us with stories of discovery of ores, boom camps, the wild life in some of these and of hardships of the trail until a late hour. Next morning he found his hobbled burro, snugged his outfit, and with a pleasant smile on his wrinkled old face, bade us good-bye.

I have often wondered if the reaper perhaps overtook him, all alone, among the hills of the desert, without a chance of human companionship in his last hour. It is pretty certain that he would pass out still searching for the yellow metal which he always hoped to find "tomorrow." I am quite confident that the anticipation of the search meant more to him and was more satisfying than the realization of a find could possibly be.

Mapping the Midland Trail, photographed below, was one of Westgard's accomplishments. (University of Michigan)

Sharp Shooting

Passing through Wyoming on one of our trips we saw an unusual number of coyotes but luck seemed to run against me, either they were too far away or I missed them though I will admit I had on two occasions a fair chance of a good shot at them. As I am not altogether a bad shot with a rifle, though no prize-winning marksman, this puzzled me until I discovered that the sight on my rifle had been bent in some accidental way. However my good wife chided me considerably over my poor marksmanship and, though I appeared to take no notice of it, this nettled me. After straightening the bent sight, of which I made no mention, I felt sure of retrieving my lost reputation.

While we were stopping for a bite of lunch in the shade of a butte, I discovered not far away, at least within easy range, the ears of a coyote just showing above a small bush. Grabbing my rifle I fired right into the middle of the bush. As I saw no animal running away from it I felt certain of having found the mark. Friend wife inquired somewhat sarcastically, I thought, what on earth I had shot at this time. I invited her to come along and I would show her. Far be it from me to boast, but I guessed I was not such a dub at shooting after all. Blithely she came along, and on reaching the bush there was mister prairie wolf, duly stretched out breathing his last, but imagine my mortification, upon discovering on closer examination, only a mangy coyote pup with one foot caught in a steel trap. The poor beast could not get away and was compelled to sit still while serving as an easy target. While of course I was glad to have been the means of putting the suffering animal out of its misery. I did not relish the laugh my companions had at my expense, especially as the subject was, as I thought unnecessarily and with undue relish, brought up for many a day afterwards.

A Town's Disgrace

At a small town in one of the western states, which I shall refrain from naming, where we arrived quite late one evening after an arduous day's battle with an exceedingly rough trail, we were very glad indeed to find a rather fine appearing hotel, though we were compelled to go to a restaurant for our supper on account of the late hour. After getting my companions assigned to their rooms and the baggage brought up, I strolled around the lobby and adjoining rooms for a night-smoke before retiring.

Hanging on the wall here and there, among heads of deer, elk, buffalo, mountain lion and bighorn sheep, I discovered several pictures of such an indecent and lewd character that in utter disgust and more than a little angry, I remonstrated with the man behind the hotel counter for the brazen exhibition of such chromos, adding that I thought the town as a whole shared with the proprietor of the hotel the responsibility and disgrace by allowing them to hang on the wall of a public hostelry.

He leeringly told me that he was the proprietor, and what was I going to do about it. He dared me to touch them and "guessed" they would stay where they were as long as he wished it, as he was the town marshal and knew his six-gun. I told him I did not intend to take them down myself, but that I would make it my business to see that they were taken down and destroyed. Next morning I was waited on by a committee of town-people and asked to forget the occurrence. The hotel proprietor they had locked in his room, as he had come to the conclusion, after much partaking of his own "snake poison," that nothing would satisfy him that glorious sunny morning but my blood. Yes sir, only real gore would appease his insulted self-esteem.

Telling the committee that I would promise to make no mention of the matter to the state authorities only on condition that they, in my presence, would remove the pictures from the wall and destroy them, they assured me that such an act would be unlawful, and anyway, the town marshal really was a dead shot, so they thought they had better not try it.

When a few days later I arrived at the state capital, I called on the governor, with whom I was well acquainted, from having made several good roads boosting trips with him, and exacted from him a direct promise that the attorney-general would take steps to proceed immediately against the hotel proprietor for maintaining a public nuisance. I learned later that this was done and the offending pictures destroyed. I should not wonder but that the hotel man, who had to pay a fine for his offense against public decency, has ever since had one eye trained on the trail and his finger on the trigger. However, I have had no further occasion to visit that corner of the out-of-doors, as I became so prejudiced against that particular community that I did not favor establishing a motor route through it.

Gates

In Western Texas some of the cattle ranches are of enormous size. Since the day of the arrival of the barbwire, these ranches have nearly all been fenced and subdivided into large pastures. The day of the open range with its romance extolled in song and prose is past. To give an idea of the size of some of these fenced tracts, it is sufficient to say that one of them, near Midland, is one hundred and sixty-five miles across in one direction.

Some of the main trunk line routes traverse several of these baronial estates and, as it of course is out of the question in that sparsely settled country to incur the expense of fencing both sides of the road, even though it may be a graded and culverted county highway, the routes are crossed at frequent intervals by fences between separate individual pastures. This condition necessitates gates. The gates are of all kinds of patterns, from the primitive so-called Montana wire gate to more elaborate contraptions that may be opened from the driver's seat by pulling a handle, depending from a long beam or be bumped open-with the front tires of a motor car.

On one of my trips between El Paso and San Antonio, we passed through a total number of one hundred and fifty-five gates, but then the distance is over seven hundred miles. Even then we traversed barely one-half of the width of this empire of a commonwealth. Of late years a new way to pass through a wire fence by motor car has been devised. This is called a cattle guard and consists of two troughs, placed apart a distance equal to the tread of a motor car. These troughs are placed above a pit dug directly on the line of the fence and a little to one side of the gate, so as to leave this available for wagon traffic. The fence is cut away entirely where the pit and the troughs cross it, thus leaving a free passage for motor cars crossing the pit on the troughs, while the pit prevents cattle from passing from one pasture to the other. These cattle guards are a great convenience.

Historic Markers

On the National Old Trails Route there are two very interesting markers. While here and there along the route where it crosses the actual path of the famous Old Santa Fe Trail, substantial commemoration stone monuments have been erected by the Daughters of the American Revolution in connection with the respective state authorities, it is the two terminal monuments which really are of special interest.

The first monument, at the beginning of the trail, is located at Old Franklin, Missouri, just across the Missouri River from Booneville. From this place the first trading caravans started on the long trek across the plains. At first in 1812, only pack-mules were used. In 1822 the first wagons, often drawn by twenty-four oxen, were driven over the trail. The journey in these early days was exceedingly dangerous. Frequent attacks by hostile Indian tribes on the caravans, often resulted in the massacre of their entire personnel and the loss of the whole expedition. Finally the Indians got so bad that the government sent troops of cavalry along as a protection and established forts all along the line. The ruins of these forts and stockades are still in evidence at many places through Kansas. One of the places where these Indian attacks most often occurred was at the crossing of Pawnee Creek. Many bloodcurdling accounts of these attacks by savage bands have been recorded, but many more are not part of recorded history, as often no one remained to tell the tale.

The old trail is redolent of the deeds of such pioneers as Kit Carson, Jim Bridger, Lucian Maxwell, Dick Wooten, and later Buffalo Bill. At many places in southeastern Colorado may to this day be seen the grass-grown trail, over two hundred feet wide, with numerous deep and parallel wagon tracks, made during the heyday of the traffic over the route in the fifties. The building of the Santa Fe railroad in 1872 caused the abandonment of the trail as a trading route. Millions of dollars worth of goods was transported over it during its existence, and it once reached even beyond Santa Fe, down to Chihuahua, Mexico.

In the old plaza at Santa Fe is the last and terminal monument of this historic route, marking its end at the old fonda, or hostelry where the travelers found a haven of rest after their arduous journey of some eleven hundred miles through a dangerous country. The old fonda is now burned and in the smoke of the fire disappeared one of the most historic edifices in the United States. Across on the other side of the plaza is the governor's palace, built in 1608, on the site of an old Pueblo ruin. This venerable building has housed Spanish, Pueblo, Mexican and American governors for three hundred years. Santa Fe is the second oldest city in the United States, being antedated by a few years by St. Augustine, Florida.

Westgard is photographed in the front seat at the California pass bearing his name. (University of Michigan collection)

Gentlemen of the Press

One of the things that cannot be avoided by a man whose work is subject to public notice is being interviewed by reporters, and of this I have naturally had my full share. Of course it is natural that local papers are keen to print things which intimately affect the affairs of their communities, and my passage through their section would generally be regarded as live news and frequently featured with display headings, the importance of the "dope" usually varying with the size of the town in which the paper was published.

Generally speaking, I have found the gentlemen of the press keen, well posted and educated men, who would present the facts as related to them with, of course, their own view on how far these would have a bearing on local affairs.

Having arrived at one of the larger cities of the southwest a few years ago I was, as a matter of course, called on by representatives of the several local newspapers. After dictating to them a statement of the facts in connecting with my trip through their section of the country on that particular occasion, I requested that care be used in quoting me literally. In justice to them I will say that this was done, but some of them could not refrain from giving expression to their impression of my personality. Thus one would describe me as burned by the desert heat till my face was the color of an old cavalry saddle, but my eyes were clear and kindly, besides which I had the warm hand clasp of a true friend. These compliments were, of course, very nice and much appreciated. But to offset them another said that I was a highwayman whose deeds were known throughout the land, and still another made the assertion that almost every city in the west was looking for me.

Evidently someone had called the attention of the reporter who called me a highwayman to the possibility of a double interpretation of the name he had bestowed on me with such good intentions. At any rate he referred to the matter in a paragraph the following day, in which he said that, of course, everybody knew that I was not a highwayman in the wrong sense of that term, but that I was a road agent.

Bad Intentions

In spite of my long rambles on rubber tires throughout the United States, very frequently into remote regions reputed to be the hide-outs of renegades, into desolate areas only visited by nomadic Indian tribes or into lands where only negroes inhabit vast swampy tracts, or sections where only Mexicans dwell, I have never been molested or even seen the sign of a suspicious desire to get unduly acquainted with my outfit except on one solitary occasion and that, as may be easily realized by those who have roamed the great out-of-doors, occurred in a city, the safe breeding place for crimes and criminals.

While we were stopping for a day and a night at a well-known hotel in one of the larger central west cities, my wife had occasion to have a check for several hundred dollars cashed, and used the money that day in a business transaction. When we were ready to pull away from in front of the hotel the next morning a young fellow with the appearance of a mechanic, came up to the car and presented himself as being the "trouble-man" or road mechanic from the factory which manufactured the particular car which I was using that season. He wanted to know if the car was functioning all right in every respect. If not, he would be glad to make adjustments and fix anything which might be wrong with it. It so happened that the car had been losing power and needed carburetor adjustment, and I told him to go ahead and fix it. He claimed that as he was going on to our next town anyway, probably he had better ride over with us and thus be able to make the adjustments while the car was in actual operation. As this was unquestionably the best way to have the adjustment made, we managed to make room for him in the tonneau seat alongside my wife.

A few miles out I invited him to drive the car for awhile so he could get "the feel" of it, and thus better determine the exact nature of the trouble to be corrected inasmuch as, of course, he was so specially well acquainted with this make of car. However, he did not accept the invitation, claiming he could "listen to the motor" better if not at the wheel. This aroused my suspicion to some extent, especially as he showed a lack of knowledge of the factory where the car was made, and acquaintance with the officers and heads of departments of the organization manufacturing it. My wife's suspicion was also aroused, and she made a point of explaining to me in the hearing of the stranger just how she had disposed of the money she had drawn the previous day. Her story, coupled with my getting my rifle unlimbered, ostensibly in order to be ready for any prowling coyote, evidently had the desired effect, because when we reached the trolley line on the outskirts of the next town the "mechanic" said he would take the electric car, and on his way in call at a certain garage, where he had an appointment to call, but would meet us at Jones & Smith's establishment, the agents for our make of car, and there make adjustment on our carburetor, as parts were available there.

As we expected there was no Jones & Smith in the town, nor was our make of car handled in that community by anyone.

The Sandstorm

In several sections of the southwest, where the annual precipitation is very light and where strong winds have for ages corroded rocks, cliffs and veritable mountains, there are large areas of sandy wastes. When an unusually strong and protracted gale prevails during the period of a long drought, the sand is swept up by the strong air current and carried along with it, sometimes for a great many miles. This phenomenon is what is called a sandstorm. At times these become more than annoying, even positively dangerous as the sand-laden air darkens the sky and like a heavy fog makes objects, only a short distance away, invisible. Not only does such a storm fill one's eyes and throat with its gritty particles, but it will sometimes entirely obliterate a trail or a road, making it difficult for one to trace one's route, besides making progress on rubber tires exceedingly arduous, if not entirely impossible.

People who have had occasion to travel between El Paso and Alamogordo in New Mexico, or between Mecca and Brawley in the Salton Sea basin of California during or after a sandstorm, will easily recognized this description. Residents around Riverside and San Bernardino, California, are often much annoyed by dark sandstorms coming over the mountains from the Mohave Desert, and so frequently are dwellers along the foothills of the Rocky Mountains in southern Colorado, Utah, Nevada, Oregon and Idaho.

The arid regions of the Navaho and Hopi Indian reservations in Arizona are especially subject to sandstorms. The white sands or shifting gypsum beds north of El Paso are as unstable as the drifts along the North Carolina coasts. The yellow sand beds in the Imperial Valley of California along the Southern Pacific railroad track burying telegraph poles, and every few years necessitate the moving of the track further east.

On one occasion when in the neighborhood of Walsenburg on the way from Denver to Trinidad, Colorado, we encountered one of these storms of an unusual severity. Our eyes, nostrils and throats soon became so inflamed that we had to cover our faces with handkerchiefs and stop the car, awaiting the abatement of the gale. When this occurred, after a lapse of a few hours, our car was embedded in sand to the hubs, our motor and inside of the tonneau literally covered with sand, and the road entirely obliterated. During the thickest part of the storm it was impossible to see a car-length in any direction, and when I left the car to investigate the condition of the ground ahead, I had to shout loudly in order to have the answering cries guide me back, though I was not more than a hundred feet away. It took us an entire day to shovel our way clear of the drifted area, in the very center of which we occupied a position like an island in an ocean.

Near Frenchman's Station in Nevada, a photographer documented a common problem encountered by many early 20th Century motorists. Cars often got stuck in muddy ruts in the roads. (University of Michigan)

Sniping Gringoes

During the turbulent conditions in Mexico in the years following the downfall of President Porfirio Diaz, the iron-willed dictator who had held the many disturbing elements in leash for more than thirty years, and brought our neighboring republic a measure of prosperity which upset its equilibrium, the borders along Arizona, New Mexico and Texas were subjected to raids by the marauding bands of various "revolutionary leaders." These raids were either instigated by bandit chiefs like Villa, for mere plunder, or by unscrupulous military or political chiefs who were anxious to bring trouble on Madero or Carranza by having the United States step in and put a stop to these practices.

Pershing's campaign in Mexico was caused by such a raid on Columbus, New Mexico, and occasional punitive expeditions were made by our cavalry, crossing the Rio Grande from Texas into Chihuahua in pursuit of raiders, who had harassed the Texas border, stealing cattle and occasionally murdering ranchers. At this time I was traveling along the border of Texas to inspect a possible route for a proposed highway paralleling the Rio Grande.

While following a poor road between Del Rio and Eagle Pass, skirting the river very closely and being flanked on the north by a chain of low hills, we heard a rifle shot across on the Mexican side of the river but, as we discovered no one in sight among the trees on the other bank, we did not concern ourselves much with the occurrence. However, in a few moments another shot sounded, and this time I heard the bullet hit a nearby sandbank with a thud and then first realized that we were the targets, and that someone was trying to snipe us. We speeded up and drove away at our best clip, pursued by a few more shots which, owing to too great a range or too poor marksmanship, failed to reach us.

On this trip we encountered every few miles one of our border patrols who would stop us and search our car for arms and ammunition, as quantities of these were suspected of being surreptitiously smuggled across the border by innocent-appearing motor-car travelers. Further down the river we found ranch houses being prepared for trouble by having machine guns mounted on the roofs of buildings and by the posting of sentries. The trouble was not only with the Mexicans who crossed the Rio Grande, but also to some extent with the great population of native Texas Mexicans, who vastly predominate in all the counties which border on the Rio Grande. These people are mostly ignorant and were easily led to believe through insidious propaganda, that their motherland was powerful enough to again gather Texas into its fold as one of its provinces, a situation which existed previous to 1836, when the Mexican province of Texas revolted and became the republic of Texas, which later, in 1845, joined the United States.

The Padre Typographers

At St. Michaels, Arizona, is located a San Franciscan mission, in charge of four padres, attended by a lay brother. This mission has been established only a few years and maintains chapels at three places on the Navaho Indian reservation. Nearby is a Catholic Indian school, maintained by Mother Katharine Dexel, and attended by boys and girls from several Indian tribes.

Father Berard and Father Weber of the mission, have taken great pains in learning the Navaho language, and have reduced it to printed form, an enormously difficult task on account of the numerous diphthongs and compound sounds of the language. A person listening to the Navaho and the affiliated Apache language spoken by one of the tribe, would be apt to describe it as a series of hisses and bitten-off consonants that could get no further than the teeth, labial sounds being conspicuous by their paucity.

These painstaking, patient padres studied the language for some years and devised special type to represent some of the otherwise unprintable sounds. By elimination they finally succeeded in bringing out an alphabet which has only forty odd letters and, after having fonts of type prepared from their own patterns of those letters differing from or being additional to the English alphabet, proceeded to erect their own print shop. Here were printed on hand-and-foot power presses the first books in the Navaho tongue. They were the catechism and a dictionary.

These constitute a real achievement and a monument to the devotion to a cause by these men of the church. As their work had to be pursued by means of private contributions, their enormous task was accomplished in slow stages and with the greatest self-abnegation. Among the most prized mementoes of my travels is a copy of the catechism in Navaho presented to me by the padres on my first trip into the Navaho country.

Texas the Great

As a young man I lived for some ten years in the state of Texas. After leaving the state twenty-two years elapsed before I again visited the scenes of my early youth, and what a transformation had in the meantime taken place! I doubt if any other state in the Union can show an equal measure of growth and forward strides in a steady march of progress.

In addition to being the biggest of our states in point of area and cross-dimensions, it had grown to be the greatest in many other respects. Thus I found on the Gulf coast the greatest business farm in the country, and probably in the world, the Taft Farm, comprising some sixty thousand acres, all in cultivation and divided into units of about two hundred acres each, under the supervision of a responsible manager and each having a substantial barn, manager's dwelling and houses for the Mexican laborers. In addition there are three good-sized towns and a private packing plant on the property. Diversified farming is pursued and a wonderful herd of registered shorthorns is maintained. The property is located near Corpus Christi and was seriously damaged in the terrible tropical tornado which swept over this region in the fall of 1919.

Near Kingville is the ranch of the King family. This ranch contains about a million acres on which are some eighty thousand head of Hereford or White-face cattle. The home ranch is a veritable mansion of white marble and would be a conspicuous estate in the Wheatley Hills of Long Island, New York, where are located so many magnificent homes of financial kings.

Not far away is the little town of Falfurias. Here is located the hundred thousand acre property called the Lasater dairy ranch. The largest herd of registered Jersey cattle in the world is to be found on this ranch. It comprises twenty-five hundred registered animals, of which nine hundred are milk cows kept in dairies, one hundred to each unit. Prize-winning aristocrats of this particular breed of bovines are here. Cows who have produced an enormous weight of butter in pounds per annum, bulls, heifers and calves, blue-ribboned and groomed like race horses.

Down at Laredo, on the Rio Grande, is the largest Bermuda onion farm in the country, the Dodd farm. This comprises over five hundred acres devoted exclusively to the raising of onions.

At Juno is located the Murrah ranch where seventeen thousand Angora goats are making their owner a fortune each year. Before the introduction of these goats into that country, the land was dear at twenty-five cents an acre, as it was arid ground and over-grown by a species of cactus, the sutol. It was discovered that this cactus, whose interior fibre, near the roots, is like succulent cabbage leaves, is a favorite food of the goats and the land values have risen to five dollars an acre in that region.

Near Austin are located the largest spinach farms in the world and also a large tract where mulberry trees are grown for the successful culture of the silk worm.

When Texas entered the Union of States, in 1845, it was stipulated that all public lands should remain the property of the state and not, as in other states, become the domain of the federal government. The proceeds from the sale of these millions of acres of public lands have for years been devoted to building and maintaining the finest system of schools and educational institutions in the country, and this wonderful work of placing the means of an education at the disposal of and within the reach of all its citizens is conspicuously evidenced by the rapid transformation of a wile-and-wooly frontier state to one of our most progressive and prosperous commonwealths.

Texas is also our largest cotton producing state and has become the richest state of all in producing oil fields. Its cattle industry is enormous, and even its lumber industry is of vast dimensions. The state is dotted with modern prosperous cities and is fast building for itself a system of permanent highways which will eventually prove one of its most valuable assets.

A Tight Squeeze

The road which now ascends from the Rio Grande valley at Socorro, New Mexico, and comprises part of the National Old Trails Route through the Blue Canyon up to Magdalena Plain, is of comparatively recent construction. The first time I was investigating this route in that locality we were compelled to make our way through the narrow and steep Lemitar Canyon, a few miles further north. At the time we were traveling in a large truck and found at several places that outjutting portions of the precipitous cliffs which formed the walls of the canyon would not allow passage of our large vehicle.

At times we were able to remove a few inches of the projections by the use of a pick, and at other times we were compelled to resort to the expediency of piling rocks near the foot of the cliff, where a projection occurred in order to tilt the top of the truck away from the obstruction as we squeezed through "by the skin of our teeth." However at one place we encountered a situation that called for a great amount of patience and arduous work. Projections occurred on the rocky walls on both sides just oppose each other, and some ten feet above the ground. The narrow space between these projections lacked a whole foot of allowing us space to pass through. By standing on the front fenders and pecking away at the hard granite boulders for several hours, working the pick above our heads, we eventually succeeded in getting through. It is doubtful if any of us will ever forget the numb arms and dizzy heads this work caused us, even though we worked in relays.

Books focused on automotive history by Dennis E. Horvath and Terri Horvath

Indiana Cars: A history of the automobile in Indiana

Hoosier Tour: A 1913 Indiana to Pacific Tour

93 Tips for Buying a Collectible Car

Cruise-in Crosswords and Word Jumbles

Cruise-in Crosswords and Word Jumbles 2

More information about their books is available at
http://www.autogiftgarage.com/bookstore/AutoGiftGarage-Bookstore.html

Made in the USA
San Bernardino, CA
13 March 2016